# CRY THROUGH
# THE PEN

# CRY THROUGH THE PEN

Fidel M. Love

Cry Through The Pen copyright © 2012 Fidel M. Love

Cover designed by Ashley Noelle Kyles

ISBN-13: 978-0615633244
ISBN-10: 0615633242

Printed in the United States of America

I cry ink…and write with tears

# CONTENTS

## SHE'S HEAVENS ONE LOST ANGEL

## CRY THROUGH THE PEN

## LONELY TEARS

## SOUNDS OF WAR

## Acknowledgments

I want to thank the people most involved in my upbringing for setting positive examples for me to follow. They instilled me with morals, values, allowed me to live my goals, and gave me the ability to dream and hope. Before, I wouldn't have thought I could be a poet, nor an author. A successful one? I owe that to my greatest supporters, who never let negative thoughts over step their bounds. Your encouragement kept me soaring high and never let my dreams down. The simplest things you've done, by showing even the slightest interest in my work, kept my confidence at a stable point. I know without confidence I wouldn't have come this far. This isn't my first novel, but it's my first book none the less. I made it! Thanks to all who pick up this book and share in the experiences of my heart and mind. You continue to motivate and inspire me.

# Introduction

Before, I couldn't have come up with a better introduction for this book than the very first poem I'd ever written that made me think more seriously about poetry. It was called, "Only A Whisper". Everything begins with something as simple and soft as a whisper. "The first rays of sunlight that inspires dawn…the pain of a broken heart that always inspires the best love song". For me, poetry began in a classroom. I wrote with a secret attraction to it, because before then I only wrote poems in the form of love letters or sweet notes of admiration during my teenage love affairs.

From there, it intertwined with my love of music and became an outlet for me. I remember sitting next to the stereo with the same cd, same songs on repeat, because I felt it spoke to me – the way music does. I lost myself in the rhythm trying to find answers to things that were going on in my life through their words. Then I grabbed a pen and started speaking for myself.

Writing gave me a voice – as it tends to do. It can take the soft whispers of the shyest person and make them as loud as a lion's roar, if worded right. Poetry, fused with thought and emotion, is a good way to bring words to life. Similarly, it makes a poet feel alive.

My earliest poems were usually things I was too afraid to say out loud. I was either shy or nervous. I had emotions heavy on my heart and thoughts running rampant in head but felt I couldn't express them properly without taking the time to write them down. For me, finishing a poem was a sighing moment of relief – almost therapeutic. Even now, I read them back to myself and can remember exactly how I was feeling at the time, and why I wrote any particular piece. It started off as a very intimate and personal release for me, but eventually became the reason for me to open up to others.

When I first thought about publishing this book, years ago, it was solely for me. It was a personal goal; long overdue. I just wanted to hold it in my hands, flip through its pages, and turn to the front cover to see my name in print. So I could say, "I did it," for the sense of accomplishment.

Along with accomplishment, came a greater sense. I'll never forget the first time someone told me my poem made them feel as well; when someone told me they'd read one of my poems online and it was their favorite. I'll never forget the time I wrote a poem, dedicated it to my friend and read it for her – when I looked up from the page, she was crying. My words brought tears to her eyes and I didn't know how to react until she smiled. She told me it was beautiful. I asked her why she was crying and she said because she was happy.

One moment that will always remain in my head, as a motivational and inspirational reminder, is the day in my African American History class. We'd been studying poets and writers of the Harlem Renaissance and given an assignment to present a creative piece of our own, representative of our culture; whether poetry, song, dance, etc. I stood in front of the class and read a poem I'd written, entitled "Little Black Boy Blues". At the end, there was a courteous applause from my classmates and when there was silence, the first words from my professor's mouth were, "Are you published?"

When I told her 'no', I felt that somewhere I had given up on my dream – but her words delivered the spark of courage to pursue it again.

When I first thought about publishing this book, years ago, it wasn't even this book. It was a collection of poems from high school, ultimately lost to a computer virus. I saved what I could and took it as an opportunity to revamp it. 'Lyrics & Poems by Fidel Martez Love' didn't sound all that appealing at the time anyway. So I wrote more, my thoughts and craft matured over time, and I changed the title to "Before & After Romance"; symbolic to the darkness and dawn of the journey of love. After much thought and revision, I changed it again to "Cry Through The Pen".

Tears are the river that cleanses the soul; writing does the same thing for me, without shedding a tear. I put my heart, thoughts, and emotion into my poetry; my trials, experiences of joy and pain. I write for me, but it is my gift to the world – thank you for reading!

Fidel M. Love
martezlv@aol.com
https://www.facebook.com/fidel.m.love

# LITTLE BLACK BOY BLUES

# Little Black Boy Blues

You see him walk a path
his peers won't go
Scared to death of being alone
but his tears won't show
So ignorant, it appears he don't know
The whole world's against him
Little Black Boy
So offensive, on the defensive
trying to prove he's a man
but so young
They'll always see him
"Ay boy, what up son..."
as a Little Black Boy
Looked down on, never up to
Always something for them to judge you
So go to school, hear the professor in college preach
Sell out or just sell his soul to the Chicago streets
You see him walk a path
his peers won't go
Scared to death of being alone
but his fears don't show
Should be scared
Ain't the least bit prepared
The whole world's expecting you to fail
Plus ya girlfriend's expecting, can you tell?
A Little Black Boy with a lil' black boy
Whose fault?
Can't teach him, what you were never taught
Don't know the Quran
and only a handful of scriptures
Show him how to walk
and maybe how to stand
but understand

there was never a Man in the picture

# Gone & Forgotten

Sittin' in a rocking chair
The shell of an old soul
but my grandmother's not in there
That's an imposters' stare
So blank and empty
Doctors say it's nothing they can do
but you can't convince me
They say a minds a terrible thing to waste
What about the minds this cerebral disease takes?
Leaving nothing behind but the shell of an old soul
A warm smile seems like its' turned cold
Memories faded, flesh numb to the tender embraces
Looks at her loved ones and can't remember the faces
Can't remember the places or the yearning to fight
An unknown element erases the journey of life
Leaving nothing behind but the shell of an old soul
Forgotten laughter, cries instead
Staring out the window
not knowing what lies ahead
Holding her hand while concealing the anger
Does she see me as her grandchild
Or see me as a stranger?
I see the shell of an old soul,
refusing to expire
A born fighter living in her last
Watching the days pass
Her stories of a survivor

## Mother 2 Be

Could a life so small
solve all her problems with really just a smile?
She's 4 months in denial
A mother to be, but she's really just a child
Her Man turned out to be a boy
but was acting like a bitch
Sick of her back and forth, lip smacking like its' his
He was 17 but that was no excuse of acting like a kid
Little girl in his face acting like she in command now
Told him to Man Up
He said, get off his damn nuts...
Then he ran out
She in a jam now
Feeling abandoned and ran down
A good girl gone wild,
thinking nobody will love her like her own child
Her mother said,
"I made the same mistakes, girl don't repeat it"
Cause she wanted to keep it
Abortion; that's worse than betrayal and treason
God put this seed in her belly for a reason
Her eyes swelling, weeping
Felt like her tears were transparent
Cause her dad was trife'
And she wasn't gon' take advice from a bad parent
Imagine her mad, staring...a young mother to be
Yelling at her own mother like,
"You was never a mother to me!"
Never remember your love smothering me
But I remember you let your ex Chuck, touch
and get under the covers with me
Feels like it's been a life full of trouble for me
But it'll be different for my child

Said, "I'll be a better mother"…then she smiled

## Roses Ripped Apart
### A Valentine's Poem

She loves me, she loves me not
She loves me, she loves me not

I stand still in a place time never passes
Thoughtless, I pluck petals
and it measures my time like hourglasses
For a pound of sand that pours
An hour has gone by
With each rose petal that strikes the grass
I've come a decision closer to my hearts' demise

She loves me, she loves me not

The sway of loose flowers on the wind
soothe the images in my mind
I fear, though I know to find a love divine
I must first offer her my heart
I sigh and moan, sometimes cry alone
that she may return it like this rose...
Ripped apart.

# Truth

If the truth hurts
then lies delay pain
Some people prefer lies
Why?
Are they sane?
Is there something wrong
with the wires in their brains?
Does it make me crazy
to want the truth?

## World Of Fantasy

She was a glamour girl
The stripper life was hardly good
Destined for Hollywood
Didn't know she probably could
design clothes
but she's taking hers off
She got a mind for fashion
but never-mind her passion
Just how big her ass is
Niggas called her 'Passion'
Walk pass'em and imagine
So that's how she would cash in
She got a degree in gaining niggas chips
Wasn't respected for her brains
just the brains that she give
She insane with her lips
Heard she made a man drop his pension
Would've called her 'Superhead'
but that name was already copywritten
She'll try anything at least once; she's not a chicken
Became a vet, but still ain't famous yet
Must be something Chicago's missing
Packed up her savings to start a second life
Couldn't make it to Hollywood
but those Vegas lights shine just as bright
The funds in her purse lacked
Plus the price of fame got a worse tax
Selling something you never get reimbursed back

She wants the finer things
Can tell she live some kind of dream
Stupid! She's a gold digger
looking for a diamond ring

She'll never find a thing
Be better off trying to sing
This is slave work; she trapped
and never heard about the caged bird
She's a wayward chick, searching on that Vegas strip
Looking for a way to quit
Wondering where her savings went
Starting over means starting from scratch
Already sold her soul, so can't bargain with that
The money's good, you can't argue with that
But then you age
and most dancers never make it off the stage
You can't argue with facts
She's not happy, the way she living disgust
So she's told to hold on with nothing to hold
There's no love in the business of lust
No friends and her new man is sleazy
Gave her a gang of freebies...her dope mayne
Cocaine showed her dealing with the pain is easy
Nobody hears her desperate cries for help
Looks in the mirror and doesn't recognize herself

## Memory Lane

No need for an introduction
The topic of discussion
Stop dancing, I'm cuttin' in
Pardon my interruption...
Unless it's on a cardboard box
with music that get the old heads bangin'
like this is hardcore rock
I'm bout to flood the mainstream
I go hard, I'm the drug the game fiends
Cocaine dreams, heroine, Christ yea!
Opium wrote for him, America's nightmare
I'm a boss, the cigar lit
Windows on the car tint
Just think, I started out on a park bench
Two turntables and a microphone
Say I've been gone a long while
but now, the nicest home
And what I'm hearing is wack
Lupe said its coming back
so where all my lyricist at?
Hip Hop Lives On
I'm only pushing 4 words
But I ain't trying to take it back
I'm only pushing forward

## Reminisce Of Home

Just take me back to a place
where I've grown and I'm known
I smile as I react to a face
Cause' I don't wanna deal with people
Who supposed to be friends
I can go home and be with strangers
who've become my closest of kin
They'll show me love
When I reach for hugs and others coldly shrug
If I'm hungry, they'll show me grub
In a place called home
They hold me up
I'll never fall alone
Although I'm gone
I've always remembered this
as I reminisce of home

## Turn To God

When my guard is down
I have nowhere to go
But I have to be a man
So it's hard to just stand down
I turn to you
When I'm faced with the opposition of death
You supply that single breath
to guide me through to find life anew

Amen

## One Day

One day we will see a rainbow
without the rain
One day we will feel healed
without the pain
One day we will see the light
and I don't mean sunshine
One day we will feel at peace
and I don't mean sometimes
One day we will accomplish dreams
and we won't be dreaming
One day we will cherish life
and once and for all, conquer its meaning
One day we will learn to forgive
ourselves, and when others are at fault
One day we will learn to love
even though mixed feelings may be crossed
One day we will learn to smile
when nothing in our lives seems worth it
One day all men will cherish a woman
and in his eyes, nothing besides her will be perfect
One day I will cherish a woman for all of the above
Today is that day
One day we'll cherish the birth of a beautiful child
And every tomorrow will be even better
If I could start the day with just your smile

## Hear Me

You hear me when I shout
Hear me when I don't use my mouth
You hear me when I speak and no words come out
You listen
You listen when I'm in despair
Listen when desperation has taken turn in my affairs
You listen when I only want to speak out loud
You listen even when I feel you're not there
You witness
You witness me as an imperfect embodiment
Witness me as a child of your creation
You witness me as one inspired
Even if my role is not significant upon the nation
You witness me as one in appreciation
You feel
At times you feel the joy that fills my heart
But you always feel the pain that tears it apart
You feel the hurt that often makes me feel used
But I share that with you
Knowing any man who is a man could fill my shoes
You teach me
You teach me that never in this lifetime will I be perfect
You teach me to love
Teach me to even love those who hate me – cause' it's
worth it
And in return, I learn
I learn through you
And through you I will learn the truth
Because you teach me, feel, listen, witness
Because you're here with me
I know you hear me

                                    Amen

18

# The Road Alone

If you walk alone in the void of dark
and the only sounds are cries and moans
And suddenly you feel apart from the world you love
Only with a caring heart can you wipe your tears
Vanquish your fears
And cast your eyes above
to catch the tear of another

Does someone care for you
if they're always there for you?
Does it make it easier when you believe?
And is the road to find true happiness, not so long
if you know you'll always have a home?

## Do I Deserve...?

When I hurt someone I love...
Do I deserve the tears?
For the mere thought
causes me to cry more than them
And this is one of my many fears

When I may break a heart...
Do I deserve the pain?

When I make someone cry...
Do I later deserve their smile?

When I say things I don't mean...
Do I deserve the sorrow of regret?

When the man I am becomes a nightmare...
Do I deserve her dreams?

When I ask you these questions...
Do I deserve your every answer to be true?
For my heart holds dear the nearest fear...
that I don't deserve you

## Cry With The Symphony

Cry with the symphony
Look in my eyes
Would you die? Would you sin for me?
If Heaven gave you wings to fly
would you send for me?
If I told you I was cold and alone
would I get a hug and your love
or just your sympathy

## In Your Eyes

Burn my inner soul
With eyes like a forest blaze
Melt my winter cold

## A Believer's Dream

I wanted the life of fame and wealth
Though coming from a life of poverty myself
I dreamed a dream
It was all I could do
Dream my greatest dream,
Hoping each night I'll see it through
Behind the others I trailed,
They thought I wouldn't excel
but I believed in myself and that I wouldn't fail
Then I would awake from it each morning
The passing days seemed to be time's warning
It was now or never for me
The opportunity to become the greatest thing I'll ever
be
I took some chances that outweighed their risks
to be able to say my dream's accomplished

# Drink With The Devil

"Let's make a deal", he told me
"I know ya pockets hurt."
But for the work, he could conceal the lonely
Put a few bills on me
but I know most of the real be phony
He smiled, said, "I frown on how you think of me,
Sit down and have a drink with me."
Something told me not to listen
What he's spitting is not his wisdom
I thought, 'I'll pass'
Till he started filling my glass with optimism
He said, "I took you out to dine fancy,
Isn't the wine fancy? I see ya eyes glancing...
Yea, she's fine, you can take her...she's eye candy."
He continued on, telling me my rhymes can be
some of the hottest and I can soar to tip the horizon
He keeps saying I'm hot, all I feel is the temperature
rising
"So sign here on the dotted line if you believing my
lies...
I mean...if you believe you can confide in me."
Together, we can rise as high as the heat
The whole room was staring at me with shiesty grins
The most unwelcoming faces, yet seemed to be inviting
me in
I signed right with the pen, immediately felt imprisoned
in walls
Saw what he filled my glass with wasn't optimism at all
Blind to the scheming, I had dined with the demons
Choking up as I seen my dreams of music drifted
lifted into the air, twisted and broken up
The bartender was a sinner, each customer was a sinner
This hustler was a sinner, waitress was a sinner

24

Just a sign that it's time for me to face the hatred on the inner
So overwhelmed by the harsh; Hell was a mirage
A lesson for those lone cries
The flames were a reflection of my own eyes
Staring into my half empty glass, I had to think to myself
Nobody's here...and I was having a drink with myself

## Darker The Diamond

Who would care to stop and stare
at a piece of darkness you wish wasn't there?
You seem to be mistaken, because it lacks a source of
light
Doesn't mean it was meant to be left alone in the
blackest night
And because in its present state, it can accumulate no
wealth
You've left it stranded to fend for itself
Because it won't dazzle, sparkle, or shine
You've neglected and disrespected it
Giving it no piece of mind
The complications, hardships, and stress that you give
In the end, always affects the way that it lives
And because you made it feel lesser with pressure
Believing it could never be better than gold
In contradiction of all negative attention
It released its natural beauty from hiding
It grew to be a diamond – from something as dark and
dirty as coal

# Beliefs

When they say it gets better – wait for that promise to come
Sometimes you'll be waiting a while
That just means every handshake and a smile isn't an honest one
Blight is the nights grin, God is righteous
It gets hard to fight this, cause' life is trifling
The eyes are the windows to our souls...so I keep mine closed
I've done things I don't want witnesses to know
Every day you are blessed, so don't hate it if you're stressed
Negativity gets you nowhere, so dedicate it to success
Music injects a potent message
It's hard to convince the youth that it's drugs
I do believe love exist
It's just hard to find the proof that it does
Death's a conspiracy to get the fraud pass our eyes
News is used to tell us our enemies and broadcast us lies
Life's a desperate struggle to keep you hunting for wealth
You pray or get preyed upon
But you can make it if you believe in nothing but yourself

## …Of The Deep

Never was I accredited my just dues
I was told I could never have as much as you
Cause' my outlook was harsh
and my skin was evidently darker
The paths I'd trend would definitely be harder
Even if I was smarter
you would try to condemn me in shallow waters
Never to know the wonders of the deep
And with the belief that I'd only fail
You'd let me trail off
with the thought that I'd only drown in defeat
You never thought my strengths would carry me
through the sea
But too long on my own
you thought I'd only found a place to die
I've found a place away from the crying
My soul has built me an island

## Sometimes I Fall

Sometimes I'm impatient, I can't wait to walk
I don't anticipate my faults, and I neglect to crawl
Sometimes I fall
If I dare to dream and at times withdraw from reality
I will awe with originality
Never regret some of the mistakes I've made
I'll take, I'll lose
Never be broken but I'll bruise
And if I choose – I'll teach myself to walk before I crawl
I'll take my chance to achieve again, each time I fall

## This Girl I Don't Know
Dedicated To Her

Whenever I see her
I wish time would move real slow
So I would have forever to admire her
This girl I don't know
All I know is she's fine and looks so sweet
I'd love her if she were mine
but it seems we'll never meet

## Walk With Me

I walked a road on which no one has trode
I walked the path with all I had
A dream, hope, and the innocence of my soul
Smile for your child
My heart never turned cold
Indeed, I froze
All alone, there was nothing to warm me
but these arms...my own
And still I prevailed, cause' I didn't stop my trail
Even though after every stumbled step
I thought I'd fail
Yet, in the end I rose to the occasion
And my life through its duration, I reign in celebration
If I said I'd do it all again, thoughtlessly
Would you care to walk with me?

## I Write A Poem Every Night

Tonight I wrote a love poem
Cause' the words just shifted and sent me
to a happy place as I drifted in memories
of when you used to smile at me
And I laughed a little
thinking of how I let your smile trap me
So I wrote a love poem
But last night, I wrote a love torn poem
Cause' I was feeling that ache in my heart
Why'd you break it apart?
I don't know if its true love or I'm just taking it hard
That reminds me of a confused poem
which I seem to be thoroughly – I need therapy
for the thoughts in my head
And poetry is what I use for'em
So then I read over a being used poem
since I've been used and abused by a few of'em
That's why I always choose never to use but soothe you
I remembered a poem I wrote about the touch of your
hand
How it had the power to turn the strong into cowards
and have them struggle to stand
Then I found a poem you wrote and one day handed me
Saying you loved knowing you could do that
and I was the only man you'd need
So I can't understand how you could stand and leave
I've wrote so many sad poems that I can't stand to read
Alone poems, I need a home poems
Lost without his own poems – and gone poems
How I need you to be strong poems
You brought a clear view to my night, I write every
night
Cause' it was a poem that brought you to my life

## Mistake

Mistake, it was to lust
Mistake, it was to bust
To only want her for sex
Haunted by the flesh
When a crush goes wrong
Come down off the rush I'm on
Lovers and friends
doesn't always turn out like the Usher song
Mistake, it was to touch and to please her
My thoughts telling me to 'Hush, it's a teaser'
Now I'm caught like I can't just fuck and then leave her
Mistake, to let her lay in my bed
Mistake, to let her stay in my head
She's caught up into how merry we seem
Now she's having those marry me dreams
Even dreams that seem as if she's carrying my seed
I'm not ready for a child, so heavy in denial
Cause' I don't want my first child to be a –
Mistake, to let her cry on my shoulder
Mistake, to lie and then hold her
as I told her everything would be okay
Leave it to fate, but its more than just two lovers at
stake

## Let Me Fly

I try to run, praying I wasn't meant to fall
20 years out of the womb
and it seems my backs' still against the walls
I'm about to crawl
As if I'm not ready for baby steps
Going through life, pursuing what's right
but I'm viewing life through hazy specs
Maybe that's why I can't see the error of my ways
through sorrows
Like the love I shake up with my friends today
won't be hate tomorrow
I'd cry from the pains I feel – the unwanted changes in
life
When closest friends become somewhat strangers by
night
I feel like I gave him the right
I dropped my guard and putting trust in him
was sorta like I gave him the knife
I pray for advice; please show me the way of your light
So darkness won't always be the array of my life
I feel as lost as a stray in the night
It's strange, they left me
The ones I trusted to, and they ain't protect me
Still I try to never let the negative changes affect me
But hate feels like love when the pain caresses me
At night, sometimes I sigh and pray
to fly away, just to try and make sense of things
I just want to get the gist of things
So I know why peace and happiness only exist in
dreams
Let me fly
Let me cry, wash away the pain inside
I want to reach for the sky

but something seems vain in trying
And I'd hate to doubt myself
Cause' I'm the only one in my corner
So I know I won't make it without myself
Give me dreams – in these dreams it's my turn to try
Give me ink, give me wings – I will learn to fly

## Hard On Shoes

I hate the way he lace'em up – this hate is tough
The way his face get stuck cause' he hate to scuff'em
When I used to be the fresh white pair
for when you would dress nice playa
Kept me right next to the bed – yea, I would rest right
there
Nights you laid ya head or got laid, gave Heaven to some
chicken
Must I remind you, till she saw me she didn't think you
was fine dude
Damn, I'm the one that helped get you her seven digits
I used to get soap and a toothbrush daily
You and me both loved to stay clean
Now I'm trapped in a closet like chapters one through
five
So you can rock a new pair of Air's that really wasn't
your size!
Since you got that lil' hook up, you gone every time I
look up
Brag on how you got'em for a cheap fee – so now you
don't need me, huh?
How you don't clean me? Still got stains from a month
ago
Oh, but you gon' stunt fa sho
Just don't think this won't come back and haunt you
though
It's supposed to be my fault cause' you're hard on shoes
Well soon, these shoes just gon' get hard on you
Don't think that I'm jockin' you though
I don't need to be seen with you – please, ya pockets is
broke
You nothing and had nothing but me, still I was rockin'
YOU though!

And you dare come to me when you needed money for a new pair?
Grabbed me from the closet dust like I was a no name –
"Yea, you there!"
Put me on ya musty feet that night you and the thugs would creep
Walking around with the slugs and heat, hitting up streets muggin' peeps
Till dude didn't want to give the ones up, so you let the guns bust
Didn't wait to see the blood drain, I ran covered in blood stains
See the shit I always go through for you, after you go do the do
You toss me right back in the closet darkness – damn, that's so heartless
I know you'z a fool, I tried to warn you bout being so hard on shoes
While you was still counting and rockin' tonight's hard earned jewels
The cops came knockin'...
I'm in the closet laughing at how fast that thug hard look went
I felt no sorrow, they said they followed the blood marked footprints
I bet now you wish you did me better – can you forgive me ever?
You don't even hear me talking – look at you, too busy talking
You'll learn not to be hard on shoes, I'll make sure you never forget
As they were about to leave with respects and apologies
I said check the closet please – then they found me with the evidence

## Hip Hop Honey

Daydreaming about her face like,
I wonder what it would taste like
Just for it to hit the tip of my tongue
A touch of it on my lips
Not much of it, just a bit
Just a dip of some of Hip Hop's honey

# One Woman To Raise A Family

Through the graces of God, she's one of Heaven's
blessings
I'm almost sure if she'd have known
she'd be doing it alone, she would've second guessed it
She could've saved her crying by telling him save the
lying
Nobody was there to claim the tears
The moment she said she was pregnant
He neglected her fears and claimed it wasn't his
Birth wasn't so sad but love had hurt her so bad
She said she would never use Cupid as a referral
The worst part was telling her mom she'd been a stupid
lil' girl
Worse than that, she was starting to throw up now
Her pounds were starting to go up
She was realizing she would have to grow up now
Worse than that, she didn't have a job to make ends
Plus with men, it was no horse and carriage
They didn't want anything close to divorce or baggage
So it was hard for her to make friends
Worse than that, she got used to not knowing a lovers'
grin
She felt like she put her life on hold – it hung up on the
other end
Asked to borrow from the father – he hung up on the
other end
So she would no longer have time for him or none of the
other men
All she needed was the warmth of her child when she
would hug him
Let him know mommy loves him...and daddy, well fuck
him
She would never let it show in her eyes

Her son would never know of her cries
Besides she was always there by his side with pride
teaching him to stride and never let go of the prize
He looked up to mom; she was smarter than any man
She'd brought him farther than any can
So the day dad tried to give him his two cents
He said, please it's a lil' too late to start with pennies
man
So you can save those comments for others
He and his dad never met again, he planned on being a
better man
Cause' that's what he had promised his mother

## Project Point Of View

For project kids who look out from the rooftops
to see a better life and realize the proof's not
in the eyes of man
To fall and rise again
doesn't really take more than what the youths got
For those like me,
who never believed this generation is cursed
And if we were, then civilization was first
For a man whose bold enough to stand and speak out
Reached out, to tell the other man
words of encouragement
Words that could lower the fist
of men who have died inside from lies and crying
Formed black hearts from nights staring at black stars
These words were to nourish it
"Bring life back to the hopeless"
He'd cherish and live life by the poetic words he spoke
with

## Rich And Poor

I hope it's not diamonds and jewels
The reason love often misses finding us fools
See I found a diamond, she shines
Just like what's within the rhyming, she's mine
I promise to give her my best and more
Rest assure
It doesn't matter what they say
Cause' we are rich in love

## Looking Back

Looking back
I should've listened to my heart
instead of voices
Probably would've made better choices
Less mistakes
Blessed with faith
but feeling like I failed my test of fate
Rejected love, embraced the hate
I loss the real; all that's left is fake
Fake smiles, fake grins
I pretend I'm spoiled
Fake vows, fake friends
They pretend they're loyal
Fake cries, inside feels like I can fill an ocean
but no tears
I don't think I can feel emotions
Looking back
I should've changed my views about men crying
If tears are the rivers of the soul
I should've cleansed mine
Looking back
I see I've been dying
with every passing day
Pieces of me just pass away
I let life slip through my fingers
Just idle or forgetful...I linger
in this place where time doesn't exist
My mind wasn't in grip
I'm a mime, struggling to fit
in a box that's just way too small
Break out of a glass cage that no one else can see
I mean, no one else but me
This is really torture, looking back I see my misfortunes

That's part of the reason why I'm only looking forward

SHE'S

HEAVEN'S

ONE LOST

ANGEL

## She's Heavens One Lost Angel

I didn't believe in angels
I had to see it with my own eyes
How she owns skies
She fly
My Queen
like if you in her throne, rise
If you can't tell just by looking
You'll never know until you kissing one
Her lips feel like Heaven
So Heaven must be missing one
Plus she speaks in a different tongue
Caught my eye like the drift of a distant sun
I'm in love with the melody of her voice
I don't want to switch to a different song
So I keep her on repeat for my health
Beauty should be shared with the world
but I want to keep her to myself
Like she's mine but she's not
She don't belong to me
She's Heavens lost angel, free to roam free
Does she know I could give her a home?
Because she gave me something to believe in
Cause' I don't think my angel is lost
You were sent here for a reason

## Dream Girl

Beautiful as ever
She could live off her looks
but chose college to get her cash right
Prettiest girl in school
but so modest, to show what having class is like
Honest
I think she was a goddess in her past life
Reincarnated, but kept everything the same
There's only one thing I would call her
if I never knew her name...
'Dream Girl'
Miss Universe
Like she just stepped out the pageant
God made her perfect
Just how I'd imagined

## I Want To Be...

Love is blind
I want to be what helps you see clear
Wherever life takes you
I just want to be there
Our love
could be the deepest secret only we share
I'll build you a sand castle
Let me be your beach chair
I want to be your sunrise
The truth amongst the lies in your ears
Free you from pain
The rain that disguises your tears
I want to be your support group
I want to be your dreams
If you believe you can fly, I'll support you
I want to be your wings
You make me want to sing
serenade you with sonatas
For lack of a better phrase
barricade you from your problems
I want to be your captain, believe you, me
can reach the limits of the sky or the deep blue sea
I want to be everything you see
Cause' if you're nothing to the world
Just know you're everything to me

## One Perfect Night

The stars would shine
The moon would be full and bright
and if the mood is right
I might cruise or bike
in the cool of night
Nice and slow
Take my time as I write this flow
Never confused about my destination
There's only one place I'd like to go –
Where ever you are
Whether North, South
You're never too far
If I happen to get lost while taking this route
The night sky painted a portrait of beauty
I just look up and find the constellation of you
And follow those stars
on my way to your heart
I stay speeding
Hope I don't crash while daydreaming
about a life me and you could share
Cause' in my dreams there's a perfect place
I wish me and you were there
We could stay the night
But my imagination is so cruel
What would make any night perfect
would just be waking up with you

## Songbird

Songbird
You sound so sweet
In my dreams I can fly
I just soar through the sky
hoping we can meet
From the sound of your voice
I imagine you look just as sweet
Everything from the color of your eyes
Lips puckered and your thighs, and your stride
like the world resides at your feet
But I could be wrong
I fear my infatuation may mislead
and I can't take another lie
Heartbreak and stutter cries, lovers die
Just hearing your lullaby
Oh my dear Songbird,
You sound so sweet
Though, you may go wherever the wind blows
Tonight, you've flown through my windows
and found just me
There's room in my heart
where true lovers lie
Where two songbirds are at home
I know every word to your song
Cause' I love your lullaby

## And She Was Gone

Shallow, once was I
Once afraid to love
Until the day you caught my eye
Passing by
You smiled but I was too shy
and I denied you a proper reply
My conscience speaks...
Quickly! Before she leaves
Don't think about it
You won't freeze, just stop and breathe
Now go over to her and speak
I would...
I wanted to wait until we could be alone
But she walked into a crowd, once again smiled
and she was gone

## If I Ever Kiss Her

To touch her lips with simple embrace
is the only urge I get when I'm standing in her face
Staring into her eyes, surfaces
sleeping emotions I'd never mentioned
but couldn't under mind
I know I'm nowhere in her mind as a lover
And I'm only in her heart as a friend
I even know about her significant other
But I only want to kiss her once, as my emotions
recommend

Softly whisper into her ears, how long I'd adored you
and she won't refuse or simply ignore you
Slowly caress her hands, finesse her body
Give her the full image of romance
Though, we both know it won't last the night
Only a minute, for just one kiss

She'll make me wait, til' the point that it aches
I know if I never get the chance to kiss her
I'll forever miss her
But I'll always reminisce of her
If I ever kiss her

# The One I Want…The One I'm With

The girl I want has a smile…
just like yours
She can compete with nature's wonders
and anything outdoors
The girl I want has this walk…
much like you
So sensual and sexy, it's a calling
If you only knew
The girl I want has a way of talking…
she sounds like you
So sweet with a tone that could soothe you to sleep
The girl I want has big brown eyes…
a lot like yours
Staring into her passionate core
There's no wonder why I see her and nothing more
The girl I want has these cute lips…
soft like yours
When we kiss
I close my eyes for a few moments of bliss
The girl I want has a body…
exactly like yours
Smooth, with just a few curves
The way she ice drips down her neck to her chest
I must've lost my nerves

The girl I'm with is nonchalant
As perfect as God could've thought
My heart sought and fought for her love
She's just like the girl I want
She's perfect for me, but I can't have two
The girl I want…the one I'm with
Glad I found them both in you

## Her Eyes

When I first saw her, I felt a fire burning deep within my
soul
And everything I remembered that moment on seems
dozed
With crude intentions, the new few minutes I was out
cold
My voice went without ode as she was about to
approach
My heart skipped a beat for each step she made my way
My mind lost a thought for each line I stumbled over
what I'd say
Seduction was all, but I swore it wasn't my fault
But I laid a path...she bit her lips and switched her hips
And I knew that path she'd walk
I tried to turn away due to some of the things I've heard
But it was her who laid her hands on me
"Passion", was her urging first word
I fell for her lure, forfeiting with no resistance
Leaving with her on my arms seemed somewhat
twisted
After a moment we were kissing
Her lips touch mine and my conscience was missing
I closed my eyes...what I saw, to nothing it compares
I was surrounded by flames, spawned by the dame
I was in Heaven, though I knew I was resting in Hell
And though I was compelled to end the nightmare,
which I couldn't despise
I endured the flames...as they were in her eyes

## Compared To You

Not the sky
Not the stars
Nothing 's more precious than what you are
Not the moon
Not the summer warmth of June
Nothing compares to the feel of you
But sometimes they question,
Is all of this really what she can do?
I answer, as long as her love remains true
Nothing on Earth compares to you

Not money
Not the threat of being deceived
Nothing could make me turn out and leave
Not another
Not a girl with something more
Would make me turn on the one I adore
Cause I love her
But sometimes they question,
Is all of this really what she can do?
I answer, as long as her love remains true
Nothing on Earth compares to you

You're a dream
You're my queen
You're the reason I say those lovely things
Your smile, the light of your eyes
Your voice, your kiss, your touch
The reasons I'd die just to fall in love
That's what you are, you're my heart
So when they question if this is all you can do
I answer, as long as your love remains true
Nothing on Earth compares to you

## A Million Ways

Sexy,
that's an understatement
It's gotta be a million ways
to describe this womans' graces
Beautiful,
that's the obvious
If Cupid aimed his arrow at her
heart, he would probably miss
Cause she's flawless, her beauty is so distracting
I can't take my eyes off her
The view to me is so relaxing
Lovely,
that should be her name
I would call her 'My Love'
and she would answer me the same
Tempting,
I feel it the moment that she passes through
Knowing the worst pain in the world
would be to want and never have you
A dream,
Or, of a fantasy
The perfect portrait painted on my canopy
I often question, "Why can't it be?"
Seductive,
from her plush lips
Her hips, such width
plus her butt lifts
Take a sip, it can be where your cup sits
She can show you the true meaning of what lust is
She can heal the heartache that such lust gives
Cause in her heart is where true love lives
There's probably more than a million ways
her essence can be defined

So when you ask me what she is...
I keep it simple and just tell you that she's mine

## As Far Away As London

I wonder if it'd still be considered a gents wish
if the first moment I'm with her is remembered through
a French kiss
She's so far away that it's only something to hope for
I cope, though my nights are lonely and I hope yours
are not cold and stormy – if I could hold you with poetry
I would...console her, I wrote more
In the darkness of a lonely heart
you can always see the clearest stars
Mine is as pitch black as space
I can see a goddess and I get that amazed
when I look at you and see that's her face
Adore mon amour with a love that will age with wine
As everlasting as our passion that will only amaze with
time
I gaze to the sky, phased at why
this star is the best I've seen tonight
and the rest just fade, don't seem to gleam in its light
I'm afraid I'll have to close my eyes and blink soon
Change comes...
I know if I ever turned away and missed a glimpse
I'd never return and be looking at the same one
I'd lose sight and the mood would defuse
Something else bad for my heart but I'm so used to the
news
You've become the star out of my speech, so far out of
my reach
As cleverly told, because you bring a sparkle to my eye
Temptation to this mans' heart, and never for me to
hold

## Goodnight Kiss

Look right in my face
Your smile brings light to my face
See it grin
Hoping the moment is never over
Yet this is coming to the sweetest end
Lips soft as the night breeze
Holding hands in a tight squeeze
Afraid the other might leave
But I won't move a muscle
except my tongue as it tangos with yours
Smooth, in the same groove as us two
I can try to pull away and savor but you'll...
give me that look that has the same effects
as the moon's gravitational pull
Staring into your beautiful brown eyes
is making my soul shake
Looking for a soul mate
but I already found mine
Goodnight – though too bad it's gone
It was a quick kiss but it lasted long
I'm catching stars in the sky
but after that there's nothing I can wish tonight
The only bad thing about her kiss
is it was a kiss goodnight

## Maybe She Doesn't Know...

Maybe she doesn't know...
that the sun won't rise without her
Dreams of Heaven don't even exist
and I'm overshadowed in my sorrow
set adrift beneath an emotionless eclipse
Left searching the abyss
for the love loss, yet once had
And the pathetic sympathetic look in my eyes
shows how even the coldhearted become sad
Maybe she doesn't know...
that my eyes water after every farewell and goodbye
I'm grieving, left alone when she's leaving
and never telling me why
She won't let me reach her,
comfort the pain she's feeling inside
Maybe she feels I won't understand, but if she opens her
eyes
The ache in her heart is the same she's seeing in mine
Soul mates...maybe we'll be in time
If I give time the time to progress
I'm trying and my heart's crying showing signs of Pro's
stress
Maybe she doesn't know...
that she fills my notepad on the days we both sad
When I cry through a pen, let it out and hope we try this
again
I can't live with you unhappy so I'd die to pretend
that my angel can just fly on the wind
Bury her stress, drop the burdens
take flight and let me carry the rest
We can cuddle together
while I soothe out the aches if anything ruffles her
feathers

## If I Could Use One Word

To explain emotions for you and the feelings that
resides in me
I could proclaim love from the first rays of the sun till
the days done
But they could simply be described in three
I love you...
If God felt you were his greatest creation, then I'd agree
Cause' the warmth of your smile washes over me like a
tide at sea
You make me want to bring perfection to every fault
You're on my mind every second, in every thought
I'd search the world and every terrain
to prove compared to you, beauty is never the same
No matter where I could go or who I would meet
The happiness you bring to my life is all the proof I
would need
I don't know if one deserves, one lovelier
I just know my love needs her

# Life To Love

Late night calls about your past loves
How they made you wept
Days you never slept
were our baby steps
But those were the old dudes
I told you as I did my best to console you
And before you knew
we were able to walk on our own two
Rarely, we planned
So barely we'd stand
You always knew how to humble me through
each step, though we may have stumbled a few
Till' it was sorta back to crawling
Due to lack of calling
Confusions and accusations
turned our smooth road to bumps
like acne patients
We knew we'd get through it
We wouldn't be the first couple to survive it
They knew we had issues, so why bother to hide it
We triumphed into a love more beautiful than before
More sure...more mature
Just more beautiful than before
It was getting serious, we needed to know if whether
we were just growing old thinking of if
we were growing apart or would be growing together
Would we get married or not, and even then
would we be together long enough to share burial plots
I need you by my side like my left lung
I don't know what I would do if you left hun
There'd be a sudden blight in living
I need you to keep that light in my vision
So together we made that life decision

# Beautiful

The glare in your eyes
The rarity in your smile
Over the years, it's something I got used to
But no matter how many times I've said it before
You'll always be the one I adore
Because you're beautiful
I remember the kindess of your heart
I miss a lot of those things now that we're apart
Being away from you is a feeling I may never get used to
But as long as you remember that I've said it before
Because you may never hear me say it anymore
I've always loved you
Because you're beautiful

## God Gave Us Angels

They don't have wings
I've never seen one fly
But they always seem to appear
from the clear of the sky
They'll stay by your side
When you feel no one cares
If you call, she'll be there
to share any pain that makes you tear
Yet, most men won't understand
and abandon her in despair
You're only a man, only a god is fearless
You do have feelings
that can be shattered as mirrors
So God gave us angels
When we're broken to shards
A real woman is there to guard
and shelter our broken hearts

## I Need You

I need to feel I have a love of my own
A place away from harm with warm arms
So when I hold tight, she'll squeeze too
I need someone to smile at
More importantly, I need someone to smile back
I need someone that I can stare in her eyes
while she glares into mine
And there, we can just disappear in time
I need someone I can hold and she can hold me
Fill the hole in my soul and make me whole
Cause' right now I feel so incomplete
And I've learned that men can weep
Since heartbreak has rendered me weak
I need someone I can call on
And she knows when she can't stand alone
I'm the one she can always fall on
The arms she can crawl to
I only need one thing in truth – all of you

## So Many Things

I can do so many things
So many things
I can bring truth to all of your dreams
I would do so much for your tender touch
So many things I could do, but all I ask of you
is that you love me too

I could dream of a world, untrue
Where everything is as perfect as you
That could never be, I already know
But my heart won't stop believing
that it's still a place you and I can go

## Angelic Dove

You bring a warm smile to my face
like the sun of summer or spring
I often dream of this love I know that only one can bring
Some prefer to gaze for days at the clarity of the sky
but I've never seen anything as beautiful as the rarity of
your eyes
When I stare at thee I can fly, like an angel or dove
to Heaven's gates but I wouldn't escape cause I'm
entangled in love
You blessed my dreams
With a gentle touch, you caressed my wings and set me
free

## Cupid Shot Me Twice

I already knew the day I said I love you
It would only take time before my love and bliss would
part
And when this gets hard
I just think of the years his arrow missed my heart
Days of loneliness, nights with tears
Darkness surrounds my heart till love's simple light
appears
And though I spurn some of my treacherous days in love
I never want to return to the way that it was
Cause' shedding tears when you're not here and crying
alone
But what's he done? When your touch becomes numb
A seductress comes
He shouldn't have struck me none
When I'm facing this predicament, it's not so nice
with the blight that Cupid has shot me twice

## A Love Poem

I should write a poem
to make the world love her
as much as I do

## More Than I Tried To Be

I tried to be
the love of her life
That night she cried to me
she became the love of my life
I wanted to hug her so tight
I strived to see
that I'd become more in her eyes
than I ever tried to be

## Only A Mother Knows

Where life begins
It's such a marv
Blessed by the touch of God
A lady's soul
Made of gold
Have you ever seen such a heart?
Covers the scars, the hurt - to give him purpose
Heals wounds that the world causes...pauses
and for a moment he forgets that its imperfect
And for a moment he believes that it's his
So he offers it to her
Land, seas, and his ribs
To know that she's a part of him
Kisses her stomach and she starts to grin
Cause' what's growing inside her is
A part of them
And he can only hope that his daughter's a twin
of the most beautiful woman in the world...
Her Mother
His Queen
His Lover
His Dream
A woman plays so many roles
Sometimes she's even an Angel
who saves so many souls
A precious gift to this Earth
until her days grow plenty old
and in her silver or gray hair
her age is simply told
She will have touched so many lives
Always kept a warm heart while some others froze
Filled with that unconditional love
only a mother knows

## Wishful Thinking

Sleepless night
Listening to the rain
Radio playing slow jams
Wondering, if you're listening to the same...
Sad music
Are you sleeping alone?
Now that's foolish
Cause' don't you know you could be in my arms
Keeping you warm
If it's cold, hold tighter Queen
And I'll hold you while you dream
Then wake you up with a kiss
Simple bliss, better believe
And if you fall in love with the moment
I promise I'll never leave
And you can have this for life
but so sad that tonight
I can't sleep, just listening to the rain
Wishing I was with you
Wondering, if you're wishing the same

## Sweet As Ever

When I think of you
I think I'm daydreaming
Cause' the whole world stops moving
and I just spend my day streaming –
Thoughts of you
Wishing we could be anywhere you like
Well anywhere...
You would turn it into a paradise
I'm scared of heights but we could climb mountains
Build shrines and design fountains
I'd like to worship you
Cover the ground you walk on with rose petals
And give you diamonds the size of gold medals
I feel like you've won
but there was no competition
Conclusions, I've come to this and...
I think you're the one
Sent from Heaven, Beautiful...beautiful as ever
And I love saying your name
but 'Beautiful' suits you better
Before I used to dream
about all the things I'd do to get her
Now I got her,
and just hoping the dream never ends
When they talk of sunsets, moonlit skies
and just staring at the view
The beauty of a summer sunrise
I know they're comparing it to you
I made reservations with your love
So I'm staying there
And if I suddenly wake up
I pray you're still laying there
Right next to me, where you'll be forever

And if it's just for one day
I gotta say that it was Sweet As Ever

## Shine

It's a fairy tales myth
but some people say exist
They say, if I ever see one
make a wish
And every night, I pray for this
That somehow I'm one of the lucky few
to truly catch a star
Beauty's way more than what we view
They say the galaxy has billions
So what's so special about one?
Well, if you took the Earth for laps
and searched a match
I bet you would find none
Quite as bright as this one
And never one as rare
So show me a billion stars
They're never gon' compare
But I don't mean stars
that they're following in the skies
I mean that special shine
that's sparkling in your eyes

# The Sleep Journey

Alone, browsing through my phone
Wishing I could dial and say,
 "Hey"
But you're asleep
And though I'd love to hear you speak
I wish we'd meet
but you're many miles away
I already miss your smile
So bright
When you grin flowers should grow
When I see you, I'll kiss you like it's been years
Though it was only hours ago –
since we parted ways, and said our evening goodbyes
Waiting at the train station
Counting the moments till you'd be leaving, then sighed
I can't even decide
if I should sleep or keep scrolling
Cause' she been running through my mind
so much, her feet swollen
My eyes getting heavy, I can't keep holding on
So I drift away into a deep sleep – no alarm
Lurking through this dream world
Searching for my dream girl
Feels like I traveled a million miles in a matter of
minutes
Cause' I finally find you – hope nothing can shatter this
vision
of beauty I'm having – so perfect it's got to be a dream
But looking just as beautiful as when we kissed goodbye
Only now we can drift and fly
Over lands, holding hands and kiss the sky

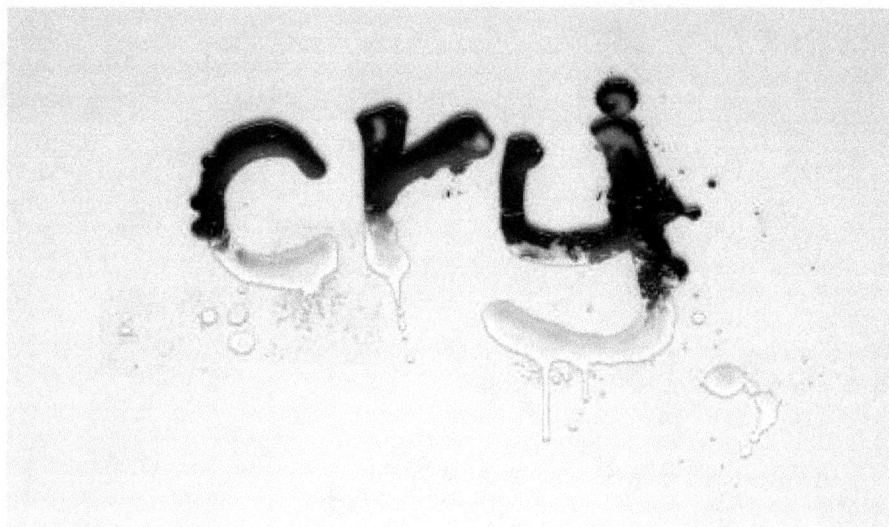

## Cry Through The Pen

The language of the soul
flows through the pen
I dreamt
of sentences, quotes
like the living notes
a musician blows through an instrument
The saxophone extracts a poem
with every breath
And I stress
to give life to this bizarre pain
Similar to the stroke of a guitar strang
If I had a beautiful voice
I would bring tears to your eyes
Bare my soul in a song
Till it appears that I have died on stage
Instead, I am alive on page
And its speech courses through my veins
How strange? A stain can complete portraits
Seeing their pain and what it does for yours
Somehow the painting is more perfect than it was
before
And the hurt seems beautiful
Never fear to love strong
The pain of a broken heart
inspires the best love songs
So if I say I never cry – it's a lie
Despite these mirrors
Reflections of my inner, every time I pen a –
Poem, verse, or rhyme
Unlocks the cages that's inside of me
Like pages in a diary
Inspires me
to bare all, despite these fears

I cry ink
And write with tears

## A Rose Untouched

A rose untouched
Before your presence beauty such as yours was
unknown
As well as the source of finesse from which you've
grown
Your unique scent has maintained since the day you
were made
We search for your source of purity
never knowing that in the sky, it is engraved
Though you remain nameless
there isn't a soul who doesn't know your look
There isn't a soul who doesn't know your style
Fearless, a child untamed, as if grown in the wild
Even after introduction to all the world's riches
You remain the worlds' only truly gifted
Because you stand strong, alone, or along with others
on soil that is never shifted by the wishes of others
You carry your own ambitions
You are beautiful the way you are
Though you are the world's most scarce resource by far
Cause' you rarity and beauty comes with a price
By the temptations of the world, you may not be enticed
The life you live, those without your grace consider
rough
They are without your glory of being a precious
rose...untouched

## A Wish For Her Heart

How foolish was I
to believe I could cast my last coin into a well
And if that alone would cast a romantic spell
I'd be granted any wish in which I compel
Or one night look into the sky, with stars in my eyes
and confess why I sometimes cry to a nursery rhyme

"I wish I may, I wish I might
have this wish I wish tonight..."

Before the night parts, alone in the dark
I make my wish to one day have your heart
I turn to the Heavens as if I have no other direction
On my knees I plead
I don't ask for much
Would it change the world if you'd interfere?
Only if you'd have her fall in love with me too
It's like I'm speaking mime
My prayers go unanswered
I'm near crying, she'll never be mine

Then something simple happens like a flower blooms
She'll smile at me tomorrow
and my infatuation continues to loom
To know one day if our love has wings
Will it be Heaven bound or forever stay grounded?
I'll try til' my last breath to have them finally spread
Maybe there's hope that it'll soar
Until then I can only place my heart in your hands
Hoping you embrace me with yours

86

# Heaven's Fallen Angel
## Two Days After Tragedy

A tear had fallen from the sky
the day Heaven's angel had flown away
But they weren't pained by her leaving
They knew she'd return to them one day
Music formed her wings
that allowed her to fall from Heaven's graces
And her voice allowed her to journey
into the most exotic places
Like the hearts of many
as she brought smiles to their faces
But The Highest Most Exalted One
has suddenly been taken
Tears of joy are no more
A shower of cries have become its replacement
For her tragic loss
You can quote a tear from every billion
She was right when she wrote it
This angel was One In A Million
I believe there is never a reason to not Try Again
So there is no doubt that somewhere
she has learned to fly again
How could the one we all gave our hearts to
simply be taken away
And for you we pray
In hopes that we'll see you again another day
You're a fallen angel, now gone
With Heaven calling angel
Aaliyah has now returned

R. I. P Aaliyah Dana Haughton
As we mourn the death of a rising star
Rejoice the return of Heaven's Fallen Angel

## For A Rose To Wither Away

For some eyes to see something so beautiful, it's truly
rare
Blessings aren't something we're all that used to
and that's why we stop and stare
Some of us may underestimate the rose
cause' we know it's always there for us to view
But that rose carries a rarity like no other flower
and that's why I only compare it to you
Even though you exist, the world can't be pictured as
perfect
Cause' in our constant revelry in things that aren't
we know that your longevity isn't certain
I know a rose that left today
So breathtaking, something took its breath away
I know nothing is put on this Earth to stay
I know that in my heart
but sometimes death feels like life's betray
While my mind's astray
I often imagine if that seed could grow old
Wouldn't it be less tragic if that were to happen?
Just to know a rose is gone – simply because it withered
away

## Gaming My Heart

This wasn't new before
I wasn't a fool before
And I've never been used
but this was before I met you
There were plenty of other girls who came
and I've always felt the same
I guess there's just something about losing
Something has to change
You know exactly what I mean
How you brought nightmares into my dreams
of living a perfect life
And honestly, I thought I could live it with you
They told me I had to be out of my mind
There was no use in making you mine
Treachery was your middle name
and no sympathy I would ever find
Why didn't I hear what they were saying
Love is just a game to her
And you shouldn't be playing

## Before & After Romance

I await the sunrise after so many dark days
Sad to come to realize that the only thing never ending
about love
is the heartache
When mere lust isn't enough to soothe you the same
And almost every 'crush' proves true to its name

I await the longing warmth after the sheer cold
disappears
Sad to realize the only warmth I know comes through
tears
When I know I've been betrayed one too many times
And I've stayed because loneliness only ensures more
crying

I await the smile of someone who'll smile with me
Sad to understand that they've also felt exiled and
empty
When you open the heart to the lyrics, not just the song
And realize that sometimes two hearts are broken, not
just one

I await the calm after the storm
Sad to look back on the past and what is gone
When I was afraid of learning but wanting to know
And so young at heart, yet yearning to grow

I await tomorrow, more rain, thicker clouds, darker
days
Colder nights or whatever is set to come
I was strong before the storm but truly after...
Now comes the dawn

# Bliss

Blissful summons
The hiss is coming
Softly, kiss her stomach
Passions longing
Caress the moment
Hearts are pumping,
a flow of heated blood through my veins
Boasting emotions
Suddenly rushing to my brain
Fail to think, and act on impulse
Scared to blink, don't want to miss a thing
From the moment we touched
the whole world seemed to hush
With utter silence surrounding
I only hear our hearts pounding
Sounding out loud
I can barely think
No exacts, only react on instinct
Unleash a primal beast from its caging
Or a sensation that takes patience
in the form of love making

## When U Don't Smile

When you don't smile,
the sun won't shine and clouds appear
Someone cries and fragile hearts shed tears
What could be so wrong to make you frown?
A feeling so strong, it will bring others down
When you don't smile,
it rains later on, the joy is gone
and even events of happiness can take shape of violent
storms
Who has deprived you of your sunshine?
The same as me, cause when I see you near crying
someone has deprived me of mine
When you don't smile,
the dark is relevant, the cold is evident
Maybe you don't know how much essence
your happiness has on each day
To have you smile, is there anything I can do or say?
I'd hate to think you wouldn't smile because of me
Or worse, something out of my hands
has taken your smile from me for an eternity
When you don't smile
You never say what's wrong
Are you just strong or in denial?
But I feel left out and without, each of those days you
don't smile
Sometimes I'm forced to believe
It's not that you don't smile...
It's just not at me

## Heaven's Wings

When the sun comes out now
The world still looks down
And I wonder how
You could be gone from here on out
Wasn't I enough? Enough that you had my love?
What could it have been
That never made you regret that day you went
This wasn't your fault, and it wasn't mine
Then who's to blame for you having flown away?

If Heaven had no wings
You'd still be here with me
If Heaven had no wings
We'd be together for eternity
If Heaven had no wings
Would there be a place for eternal peace
When my soul couldn't go on
Would there be a place for me
If Heaven had no wings
Some nights I wouldn't cry, wondering why
You could...but I couldn't fly

What didn't I know about you
That made me deserve living without you
I knew you always cared and one day you wouldn't be
there
Despite the love we shared
One day the sun would arise to a damp and dreary sky
Tears in my eyes, I'd curse our demise
Maybe I should try to view this from a different angle
There was no way you'd be here forever
This world doesn't deserve an angel

Where have you gone, no one will let me know
You said our love was forever, I shouldn't have let you
go
How is it possible to live a dream
When I no longer dream of beautiful things
And has taken my heavenly dreams
No one is destined to stay
One day we'll all be carried away into dreams...
On Heaven's wings

## On Our Own
Dedicated To The Departed

If I have to leave you tonight
won't you remember me
for what I was in your life
And promise me you won't cry
If there's the chance I won't return
You promised me to stay strong

I know I'll be weaker without you
And life will seem meager without you
But I won't be alone
knowing I have you faithfully at home
And I can find it in me to go on, on my own

I don't want a tear in your eyes
Knowing I could be gone by sunrise
I won't answer when you call
I won't hear your cries at all
And I know I won't make it back by nightfall
If by night you should turn cold
My arms won't be there to warm you
But promise me you won't turn back on this road

I know you can do it, if I can
My heart will see you through it
No matter what separates us
Forever in my heart, never will you be alone
In the depths of solitude of dreaming of you
I could make it on my own

# One Night

Can you make love without being in love?
I think I can if it's done right
So one might, think of what I can have her feel
if I was given just one night
Have her body twitch like I was pinching her nerves
when I'm only kissing her curves
Know the secrets of her soul
when I zone deep in her eyes
So I can satisfy her every measure of pleasure
when she moans deep and she cries
Never felt a touch like mine
You feel a rush, still and hush
Forever true, never knew of anything as real as us
Lost in the moment of lasting passion
Satisfaction is the only cost of condoning
One night
of trusting a stranger, lusting a stranger
Never thinking of how touching can change us
or where we'll be tomorrow
Will we be as hollow or bleed the sorrow
of sharing just one night
Well I guess we'll see tomorrow
For now just touch and caress me, lust and undress me
If you don't say the night
make sure you stay right next to me
Sketched in my memory with the best of my imagery
I bet you'll remember me from just this one night
So let's not stall and have a moment of waste
Since I saw you I wanted to taste
Let it all fall to your calves
This one night just might be all we have

# A Kiss She'll Never Get

I close my eyes with the hope of approaching
I try to calm my heart, cause' now it's boasting
Beat after beat, as we slowly come closer
Massage my lips with my tongue for its moisture
Could they ever feel as soft as hers?

There's a moment for one last look in her eyes
Wondering, what kind of passions will arise?
Will I never want to open my eyes,
lose track of time, keep her forever in my mind
And never want to say goodbye?
I can't wait till her lips touch mine

My eyes close slowly as I draw nearer
Suddenly I can't hear her, feel her
I see me and her in the reflection of a cried tear
Only if she truly was here with me...
I see clearer, as momentary bliss diminishes
We finish the kiss, and wish it wasn't just to a picture

## A Tear Falls Slow

The hurt that has you ask the unanswerable why
makes you sigh
And the sorrow that hallows your insides
has your soul cry
Whenever that pain begins to show through your eyes
Everyone knows when the pain hurts the most
Cause' your tears fall slow
Too hurt to cry out
Lost in a void with no noise
The pain never dies out
Maybe one tear falls slowly
And as the drop disperses, it still hurts
And curses another note in sad verses
Another chord as your mourn, humming life's sad song
Or is it swallowing before wallowing in pain – to cry no
more
Though they already know how much of that pain
resides
It shows in your eyes the most
when your tears fall slow

## Bad Thing About Dreams

I fell asleep, not to debate my shallow aches of today
It was nothing as I had dreamt
Simply...it was too empty
Cause' she was no where I had went
I know it's my obsession
but without her, nothing precious is ever in my sight
As depression begins to lessen, I bid myself goodnight
At my first sight, the lights begin to fade
Reality drifts away,
I hear her voice calling my name
I see her smile, her glaring eyes
Her tempting flesh, I'm tempted to feel
And I am soothed as we touch, her aura changes moods
Yet, my wounds never heal
And I believe that's the only bad thing about dreams
Each time they're summoned, it's only for a moment...
They're never real

# What Do You Think Of A Grown Man Crying?

What do you think of a grown man crying?
Is it as sad as the sight of a lone man sighing?
Or does it remind you of an old man dying
He has suffered his share and now being relieved of the pain
Heaven has made death like his tears
So he is just in need of the rain
to pour from his eyes and wash away the aches
His sores like shores that get washed away by lakes
How do you judge a grown man crying?
Is he viewed as a shrewd that's wept cause' he's defeated?
Or seen as a King that realizes there is only one God
Understands he is just a man and has accepted his weakness
As a man and nothing lesser, I take pride in my manhood
But under this pressure I've cried like any other man would
I tried to keep it inside but the burdens on my soul you can see
Just look into my eyes as they begin to roll down my cheek

# Sad, Sad Man

I see people watching and try not to stare back
What are they whispering for?
I'm not that insecure so I take out a smile and wear that
As I pass them by – I want to ask them why
But there's no need, the words linger like an everlasting
cry
"He's so handsome" – I smile a little cause then they say
"He's going to make some girl a fine husband someday"
He doesn't have money yet, but that's going to change
He'll have a cash flow better than the one going through
his brain
flowing from his pen and onto a page
Money will form from those poems, it won't be long till
those days
It's like he's destined for greatness; can't you see the
shine in his eyes?
So I'm always trying to comply
I'm doing fine as long as I can keep them blind to the
crying
It's easy to fool watchers – they'll only see what I show
And half the time they're only watching just to see
where I'll go
I never take them down that dark path, so they see what
hides there
I realize that only few lives care to know what really
resides there
When I take off this cloak and the mask and lie bare
They see a look of hopelessness and rash
See my dreams being spoken and laughed at
My spirits broken and half cracked
I don't always feel as handsome as these pretty girls say
I feel as ugly as these streets

and sometimes you gotta be – that's this gritty world's
way
I can't wait to be paid, some days are gray and I hate I
was made
I hold onto my faith and prayed but off a righteous path,
I've strayed
I'm trying hard to reach that destination – don't look
back
Stay focused on what's ahead and hope the rest will
straighten
I've been blessed but I'm still waiting, some of them still
hatin'
The rest still debating why I walk around like I had bad
plans
Can't see through the mirage, underneath the fraud is a
sad, sad man

# Birds With Broken Wings

Whoever said birds with broken wings don't fly no
more
Just bandage me up and I'll try and soar
Just like the spirits of soldiers don't die in war
They live on – so the kids won't cry no more
Nor undergo the hardships we tried to abort
Different lies, dreaming of distant skies
but we're blinded by poor sights
It's confined us to poor sights and hopes for the future
So what would you do if you were another bird with
broken wings?

I'd pick up this pencil and paper
and try to write more – cause life's more
than plotting my next swindle and caper
Life's a bitch
But I can't keep pretending I hate her
Though sometimes I just want to say fuck it
like I was intending to rape her
Please give me just a minute to savor –
One peaceful thought
So I may stray away from this sinning behavior
And pray to God that I can send in this favor
Guide me to the light
Provide me with the sight to envision a day of –
miles full of places for building a new start
So we can see more smiles on the faces of children
Less tears in the eyes of our mothers
Less clouds and more sunshine in the skies above us

## New Direction

Lost, that's how I describe it
The feeling of being tossed aside
The strive gets harder just to try to survive it
Walk around lost, strayed from your road
Such a long ways from your home
Things you've grown accustomed to
And the things you've known
It's gone in the distance
Leaving you alone, defenseless on a mission
to wander and find your way back
Wander like blind or stray cats
Never questioning if you'll fail
Forget that old path
Sometimes it's life suggesting a new trail

## Black Rose

Beautiful Black Rose
So rare
Attract those who stare
but their feeble minds
would never understand
enough to compare
your beauty to something else
Could it be I believe in a myth?
You transcend the bounds of nature
Or you don't even exist
They are so numb, so nothing's felt
No tears shed
The day you began to die
So mellow
and rose petals began to appear red

# Mime

I wrote the greatest love song, then forgot...
Nobody will ever hear my song
I'm alone in this box

Listen to Wayne's No Ceiling
and wish that my limit was the sky
But my limit is as high
as my arms can reach

Loneliest place to reside, I'm still here
But this is not make-up over my eyes
These are real tears

Only time and fate gon' tell
So I been waiting –
holding my breath so long, my face turned pale

I get frustrated, sometimes ticked when you pass
And I'm screaming as loud as I can...
Damn, how thick is this glass?

Why can't anybody hear me?
I'm choking up – Am I the heart of a joke
Nobody told me
I wouldn't get far with this rope
Tug of war but going nowhere, the harder I pull
Just a clown on display – the heart of a fool

Loneliness may just be a part of my role
Nothing to fill the emptiness in my heart and my soul
Life's moving fast, nobody bothers to slow
down,  to see my frown
Maybe they just think it's part of the show

## Question Love

I cried to mi amour
Am I wrong not to trust love
if she's lied to me before?
I don't know how to love
So sick of shallow love
so I tried to reach the core
Go deeper than her features
I tried to be much more
Her equal
So any problem I have, she's got
So I can never be happy, if she's not
Going through a trial in denial
Saying she's fine
but she's lying
I'm so in denial
Holding a smile, while she's crying
And while we talk about the future
Saying, I'm the perfect man to suit her son
And you can be my daughter's future mom
Who's to say we'll still have love when the future comes
Sometimes I question love
I been so crushed in love
When you give everything
trying to make something out of nothing love
Then make the same mistakes
I guess I didn't learn much from love
Except never say forever
and never say never
Now, how long do you think this love will last?
I know what you're going to say
Maybe we're loving too fast
and missed something important along the way

Lonely
Tears

## Lonely Tears

You could never tell if you look in my eyes
How it feels to be as lonely as I
I could cry
but my tears never show
I just silently sigh
and listening ears never know
Defiantly lie
Cause' I don't think they listen regardless
When I tell'em she scarred it
Borrowed it
They just see me as heartless
How long must my soul suffer
I'm not a selfish and cold lover
Just take the time to see
where my heart is
It's probably abandoned and smothered
Still in her hands cause' I love her
But she's in the hands of another
Smile, bury my burden
Says the bearer of pride
Hide the hurt, its better inside
So the loneliest tears
are tears I never cry

## You Remind Me Of Pain

I'm dying inside
Somebody call a medic here
Worst pain I've ever felt
Never had the chance to shed a tear
I can't cry, where's my nerve at
Cry over you?
You don't even deserve that
Wish you could take the words back
The hugs too
'I love you's'
I wish I never heard that
Just blinded me
for something I never seen coming
Because of you
I think those words will never mean nothing
I'm not mad for what it's worth boo
I just regret the moment I first kissed you
When you left
You should've took the hurt with you
Now that the feelings of love
have been replaced with pain
I'm trying to erase my memories of you
and hope no trace remains

## I Don't Wanna Be Alone

She don't see I'm a on mission
I know it used to be every night positions
and stomach kissin' but now something's missing
This woman's pissed and – she don't wanna hear
that me, I want a Lear
and she just wants me here
She just wants my ear
so she can whisper into
Maybe I can kiss her and do
things that'll have her body shivering through
Send chills up her back
But I'm trying to build up my stacks
so we can build up our shack
Turn this house into a home...so I'm gone
I'm out and on my own, you on the couch and all alone
You feel like a fool!
Plus all ya girls say I still like it loose
So suddenly, you feel like its true
I'm out chasin' more than my dreams, is what it seems?
But its nothing more to me, all I adore is my Queen
I'll want her if she goes –but she's won't
Cause' I want her even mo'.....everyday!
I just wonder if she knows

## Always

Me and you are no more
That's what I'm thinking as I wrote this track
I'm still trying to cope with that
Memories of both us back
when everything was kosher
Sex, I used to coach her
Remember everything I showed ya
Remember you would cry
I was your shoulder
Every conversation that ended in goodbye
made us closer
The heart grows fonder
but still I made this tape for you
to say I'll wait for you
but I hate being away from you
There'll always be a place for you
You hear I'm next to shine
Wherever I lay my head
There's your pillow next to mine
Sorry, we lost touch but you're never underneath that
You'll always have a friend
Just reach out and I'll reach back

## Be With You

If it can't last forever
We goin' through a storm
Don't mean we can't pass the weather
Can't laugh together
Can't be friends again
My hearts broken, but it can be mended
Let's not pretend it can't...
I love you, did I mention
If you gone, I can love you from a distance
If you happier in his arms, that's fine with me
If you meant to be mine, only time will see
No more crying to sleep
That's all I can say
He do you wrong, I'm a phone call away
And that's not a threat to him
Just means I'll always be there for you
Care for you – no disrespect to him
If he don't live up to what you expect from him
Understand that he's only a man
If we could abort the abortion
and try to be a family again
It would be his and her everything
I'm kissing her in every dream

## Wish You The Best

I end up being humbled again...it was fun to begin
So should've known it would come to an end
Guess you can't get from me
what you wanted from him
And I don't want it to end
See my whole world crumble again
Gave you my best, he gave you better
That's life, don't stress her
No choice, but just forget her
like it's whateva
If it's meant then it'll work
but I'm sick, pretending it don't hurt
and what's worse?
I didn't even hear it from you
I called you just to hear if it's true
What you tryin' to prove?
And you crying, how you ain't got the time
and maybe you was lying
but baby, who are you lying to?
I want you but I don't need you
and yea, maybe I love you
but I could leave you
Better yet, you left me
Til you come back, I'll miss you to death
But if you don't, I just wish you the best

## Where Do Broken Hearts Go?

Where do broken hearts go?
The same place memories fade
A dark lonely corner
where our chemistry strayed
Young lovers turned old friends
Hearts frozen in the cold winds
Bitter, fighting against holding grudges
Against my better judgement
Still wondering where the love went
The love that didn't exist
Just between us, as if we've never seen lust
Vowed that we'd stay a secret
Slept in secret, kept the secret
So when you left, I wept in secret
Starting over is getting to know you again
Having to see you as an old lover, new friend
Please tell me you remember the lover
Before your heart mentions another
Dig deep, find what it was meant to discover

## Do You Think About Me?

Do you think about me...
like I think about you?
One cup's not enough
I need to drink about two
to drown all my problems
and kill my thoughts
Numb my soul
So I can't feel my loss
I'm so used to being a winner
Not used to this weather
Losing's my winter, I use this as shelter
It wasn't just loving her, I felt her
Touched my heart
When you left it from dusk to dark
Where'd my sunshine go?
Wish I could see her leave again
just one time slow
You disappeared like you never were there
Could've warned me...
I would've been better prepared
for the day I wouldn't have you
Gave you everything from your dreams
to your castle
I thought I wouldn't have to
prepare for that
I thought about her as wife...my wife
Then you walked outta my life

# Where Does The Pain Go?

Sometimes I look at your pain like it's strange
I don't believe you're hurt
Where did we change route?
Born from the same roots
But I wasn't grown from the same tree you were
We both sprouted from humanity
Both a part of the human race
So why? When I see tears from your eye
I stand and watch with an inhuman face
Like I don't understand or comprehend
your pain...I can't feel within, I can't pretend
So I may dry your eyes and wonder why
you and I are different
If I have cry-less cries
Or maybe I just cry inside...

## Hopeless Romantic

Is it so obvious that I'm a hopeless romantic?
When it comes to falling in love, I'm too frantic
I admit to mature feelings
And emit emotions I'm not even sure I'm feeling
Then I start to think about her
and think about her more and more
Stand in awe once I find her flaw
and she's no longer what I was looking for
But before love could bloom, my heart gave birth to it
She was too perfect, why couldn't I nurture it
Was it me and my fear of ever getting too close?
Or my fear of believing
and having it not turn out to be what I wanted the
most...
TRUE LOVE

## My Ballad

My world hasn't been the same since
Baby girl graced it with her presence
And her smile completes the void in my life
I'm not sure if I'm supposed to say this
I haven't given time for my thoughts to weigh this
But I wish she came to fill the emptiness of my heart

And I sing a ballad night after night

Only if her ears could hear me
The things I'd say would make her fall weary
And maybe she'd fall in love with me too
If only words could reach when we're this far
I would for you and you would forever have my heart
Not even the world's limits would be too far
Our souls would never truly be apart

And I sing a ballad night after night
Hoping your love would transcend the light
And I'd wait a lifetime...
for my whispers to carry on the air and take flight

## Letter To My First Love

I wanted to write my love a letter
but was never sure of everything I should tell her
When you were mine, I was blind but now can see
the reasons I was crying that night from my balcony
We made a promise to each other
Not knowing they were ones we couldn't keep
And when we were apart, was I the only one who
couldn't sleep?
And when we had to say goodbye, neither of us wanted
to speak
Fear of breaking the roots of a love that was running too
deep
When we were holding hands,
anyone who caught a glance knew I loved her
Had my chance as her lover, til she fell into the hands of
another
I reminisce on those days that I miss
The summer we shared – our very first kiss
The last days we kissed and every kiss in between
Now every time I wake up without you it's like I'm
missing a dream
I didn't mean to desert you, I'm crying here
Nor unintentionally hurt you
Now, I know where you found your silent tears
Since you've been gone, I haven't really been alone
But I mourn when I read your old love letters...
And wonder what the case could be
Looking at pictures of my love where your face should
be
I hope your heart will always have a place for me

# In My Heart

I can see your reflection when you're not there
Just close my eyes and stare in the dark
So know you'll always be in my heart
I can feel your presence, even when we're apart
It's hard to explain...it's as if you're right next to me
I get that same feeling
Slowly going down my spine
Whenever you're on my mind

# Where Broken Hearts Lie

At the start of every love letter, anticipation rest
With a vigorous pounding in your chest
You're willing to put your heart to the test
But not of how strong you are
Rejection is pass or fail
Will you be alone tomorrow?

At the beginning of every crush, it's like fantasies for
hire
Nightly dreams of the one you admire
They become your one and only desire
Her face is imprinted in your mind
With her love divine, will she ever be mine?

At the end of every kiss, you've transcended to a world
of bliss
Heaven has granted you at least one wish
with the sweetness of their lips
Even if your one wish wasn't that one kiss

At the end of every love, there's pain and no more hugs
You only feel comforted because the rains are tears
from above
Even with the reminiscing pain inside
You don't have to reside where love dies

At the end of you and I...
I don't know what there is
Tears, no desire, no one to admire
No one kiss, a forsaken wish
Where we cry our love dies
It's the last breath of unspoken goodbyes
Where the sorrowful sigh...where broken hearts lie

## I'll Never Meet Her

Thinking of the countless days I spent
wishing for a soul mate
Cause' everyone has a soul mate
But for them, are you suppose to wait alone
or with someone else
Cause' it pains to be by yourself
Before I knew she existed
Her face, I'd already seen
She was as beautiful as can be
I'd dreamt of her in a dream
Nothing like the cover girl of a magazine
Or the seductress on a Hollywood movie screen
She had beauty you wouldn't believe
You wouldn't believe she was meant for me

Then came the day I saw her
She'd finally arrived in my world
Due to countless days of planning what I'd say
My mouth was deprived of words
Hers wasn't, politely she said hi
Overly shy, I barely managed to smile
We stood idle for a while
She left with an uncertain sigh
I couldn't even say goodbye

## Rejected

I don't know how much rejection my heart can take
I constantly place it in your hands, fearing it'll fall and
break
Sometimes I doubt that you even care
I know I'd be much happier if my feelings for you were
never there
Then I wouldn't have to face my thoughts that haunt
and taunt
But it's so hard to just turn away from the things I want
And the things in my heart
I told you what's in my heart is you
But you just rip it apart, and I don't know what to do
I wonder if the one you do love is something of
perfection
He must be...he didn't have to face your rejection

## I Tried To Be...

I tried to be...
the love of her life
I lied to me
I believed I could be the love of her life
I wasn't her type
I knew that before we knew each other's name
and it haunted me
She wanted me
but I could never be what she wanted in me
I tried to see pass that I could only be me
But the me, underneath is a child too lonely to see
Homely with grief
Cause' I tried to make her happy
Cried the day it happened
Our happiness together just wasn't to be
No more emotional change ups, disappointing hang ups
I tried to believe it would change but...enough of the lies
At least I know that I tried
But I will never be the love of her life

## Something Of Mine

Today, I think I'll write her
just to tell her I'm doing fine
Still doing rhymes
And if you don't mind...
I think you have something of mines
You know I hate to ask, but I really need it back
And no, it's not the music I left in your CD rack
You can hold on to the slow jams
I don't think I'll use them ever
They only make me cry and sigh
seeing how you and I used them to make music together
And I gave back your diary just as you requested
You returned my book of rhymes so I can fill it with
confessions
My pen spilled with depression
the night you sent your friend with a checklist
of things I should return
And she told me you were giving back my necklace
There was nothing I could say, after all we both were
through
I asked you to please keep the love letters and poems I
wrote for you
However I do think you still have something of mines
you haven't sent me
My heart...since the day you left space in my chest has
been empty

## Miss You

Now days it seems harder to cry
Though I look at old pics of you and tears water my eyes
We can't even talk now, our words just barter for lies
Saying I'm doing good, like I'm glad we can start our
new lives
I'd rather have my old one back
How'd we come from friends to lovers?
Now it's over, so where do we go from that?
I can't stand you not calling me 'baby'
So I just stopped calling
Cause' something inside said to keep calling is crazy
You were my better half and I don't feel wholesome
now
I got so many empty feelings
So I took'em and wrote some down
Made sure I always got this statement in
and addressed it to you in a letter too late to send
You rarely see me smile now like I hate to grin
I feel like I just loss one of God's angels
So how do I tell him that and make amends
And hope I am one day blessed with your presence
again
And forgiven, for I'm a man and so stressed with the
lessons of sin
With you I was blissful, not to be taken as a missed truth
I miss you...

## Lonely

From the seconds I couldn't see
to the moment I didn't need
I never thought I would believe...
I could feel alone
My days grew colder, the nights grew darker
Chivalry would fade and misery found a way to stay
I couldn't understand how anything I could've done
could condone me...to a feeling so lonely

When I think of the pain no one has sent me
I'm torn by the irony of feeling so empy

# Rain

Lately no one has seen me on the brightest day
Cause' I won't be returning to the natural world right
away
I prefer the dark; it suits the condition of my heart
But don't think that I'm so strong
cause' you've never seen my pain have me cry
You have to understand...
that isn't always the rain over my eyes

## Mistaken For Rain

I understand if you're confused
As much as I was after the delusion
As an illusion, she was sent forth
Then again, that's what those tears were meant for
I do my best to hide my pain
Never show my shame of falling in love
Although it hurts with my heart being taken in vain
They'll never know as long as my tears are mistaken for
rain

With the rain falling in a million drops outside
I have one excuse to stay locked inside
As it pounds heavily against my window
My tears revel in the revelry of my sorrows
With every tear I allow to flow
When will the pain suddenly go?
Cause' unlike my sorrow
Tomorrow, it may be dry
And a tear will still be in my eye

I walked alone through a storm, wandering without a
home
Cause' if a home is made on love
I'll never return to the place my heart was torn
Crying alone, I was on my own
I felt no one would ever understand
No one ever paused to lend a helping hand
I learned underneath the rain, no one worried about my
cheers
Underneath the rain, I had no tears

## Tears Of The Past

Touch,
Wondering if to kiss her is worth it
when past canvas teaches that cause it's beautiful
doesn't mean the picture is perfect
Maybe the heart's broken, reasons I'm losing focus
and I don't know how come
So I'm looking back on us like an old photo album
Proofs of everything happiness...perhaps not
Only a snap shot
Picture you smile, picture your laugh
Picture me enjoy the time frame
Cause' I'm not always sure it's something we'll have
Like how I know I won't see your face today
and notice the clearer images begin to fade away
I wonder if it's only a smear in my lens as my eyes
cleanse
and you begin to reappear with other men
I don't want to know...
I don't want to blame him for our portfolio
Wish I could change film but it's something I've tried
before
Realizing what you told in a fake pose, and you've lied
before
So can I ever love another, close the cover of 'Tears of
the Past'
It's a new page and too late, those tears should've been
cried before

## Unnoticed

At times I've been hurt by the ones, I want none closer
and shrug it off, love is soft...love is loss
I'm a con, a poser...and I only turn to a poem for closure
I write numb in core, so I find none amore
as tears fall mirror image as the ones before
So I'll smile with pride, hold my head up high
not to show that I care
With a broken heart, soaked let tears flow in the dark
Hopefully no one will notice they're there
Though at times I feel beaten inside
I know these insecurities can eat me alive
Yet, people say Prolific is a soldier, strong
and never know the foes of my soul, cold and alone
Each night that I mask the pain and ask for rain
Cause' things I thought couldn't last would change, have
remained
So I smile with pride, hold my head up high
not to show that I care
With a broken heart, soaked let tears flow in the dark
Hopefully no one will notice they're there

## Old Letter

I read an old letter, I'm ashamed to say
Some of those memories of the past
I couldn't completely stow away
Actually I sat a minute and read a few
The first of them were love letters sent from you
Then I came across one, my heart dropped and I sighed
You wrote about how you loved me so much
And how I made you cry
Then there was the last letter you gave me face to face
So I'd know you'd be leaving but our feelings wouldn't
be erased
Then I found a clue in a letter you sent through a friend
You'd betrayed me in those letters
And I shouldn't hope to see you ever again

## Boo, This Time I Promise

I'm not sure what to believe
when it seems you place everything above me
The "baby, I'm sorry" or when you tell me you love me
The nights were I'm hoping, hopeless when I haven't
spoken to you
Missing sleep each time you say you'll call but never do
You take a piece of my heart, scarred
but not yet broken in two
I only want to cry when I hear your sweet voice only
beget lies
Cause' I miss times of homage till you say
'Boo, this time I promise'
For you, my love and interest only tends to mount
Upset enough to shout when you don't keep your word
And with my stress goes doubt
Knowing you've broken promises before but I didn't let
those count
I cried, knowing I was in love with a voice that only
begets lies
Cause' I miss times of homage, after she swore on our
love
and said, "Boo, this time I promise"

# HEARTBREAK

Having trusted someone whose sole purpose was to
deceive you
Every time they'd look in your eyes just to lie, so you
can say, "I believe you"
All you wanted was to build a relationship with
someone on a love that's strong
Right when you felt you had found them, that love was
gone
Truthfully, you knew the love was never there
But it seems so hard for you to find someone who'll ever
care
Really you only wanted to be touched than left forever
bare
Easier to find love inside a lie, cause you know life is
never fair
After the promises of cheers, pain of dominance and
tears you wish to end
Keeping the pieces of what's left of your heart to
yourself seems best
cause' you're afraid to take that risk again

## Simple Words

Why is it now I can think
of everything I never thought to say
But back when I could've fought to stay
I was speechless when she walked away
I go over that conversation repeatedly in my head
Wondering if she'd still be with me if I said –
something as simple as 'I love you'
Wait, no that should follow the notes
as I quote what was wrote in the most romantic novels
But that's not what she wanted to hear
She wanted me near
She never wanted the fear of me
leaving her with the loneliest tears
So emotionally distant, she would come to hate it
It was just so complicated
When it could've been so simple
It made no sense boo
We ruined that most beautiful thing God made
since you

## It Never Rains In The Desert

A lack of peaceful thoughts to humble me
I'm so stranded
Dammit, abandoned
Look into my soul, you can see the tumbleweed
I'm isolated – and I so hate it
that I feel the blessings went and a desert sent
me to place inside so desolate
I used to feel alive
I used to fear to cry
I fought to live through and survive the drought
Try to welcome each day with new light but I rise in
doubt
Just when I was hoping I can smile today
My spirits raised
but it seems the nearest face is a million miles away
Or is that I only want to look into hers?
I still remember the echo of hurt as my ears took in the
words
I didn't know if it was better to be alone here than die
So I cried that night and that night my tears ran dry
They say, I'm going to rot in vain
Release it, don't stock the pain
You can't stop the rain
I can't hide, being a loner is killing me
but it's better than them knowing my vulnerability
Overpowered by lies
The terrain is showered with cries
A warrior none the less
But in fear of a broken heart inside, a coward resides
I seem to have no ability to rebuild, I lack this
I'm torn inside, so to keep them out
my exterior is covered with the thorns of a cactus
I know its dumb right – but some nights

I sit and wish I didn't lust, wish I could trust
Had someone I could kiss, I could touch
When I did, I just couldn't let her in
She fought wars to understand why I couldn't let her win
She wanted my secrets but that's farther than the trust last
So anything deeper for her would've been a trespass
I thought alone, I'd cry less
But I'm just condoned to silence
The root of others evil has grown too strong in my mindset
I feel so torn inside – like what's wrong inside
I don't really understand what's going on inside
It's been so long since I mourned and cried
I feel a warm drop roll down my cheek
Suddenly, it feels like the pain has been severed
This is strange as ever
Cause' it never rains in the desert

# What's Love?

Loneliness
Obsession
Vulnerable
Emotional

## She Meant Goodbye

She put her arms around me and her hug seemed kinda
loose too
Deformed of its warmth, it wasn't the love I'd been used
to
Yet I had been so longing for her touch
I'd still reject and regret more
With such a numb feel, it was unreal
We didn't want to hold each other
but neither wants to be the first to have to let go
I could've shed a tear as she went
Cause though her words were of endearment
It was clear what she meant
Curious to death of when will I know the blessings of
her affections
So I kissed her on the cheek, it was cold for reasons
other than the weather
Not even a wish for her lips, and I answered myself,
"Never"
Will I ever see you again? "So I guess this is goodbye...?"
She wouldn't even look me in the eye and said, "Yea, for
tonight."

# I Don't Wanna Remember

Do you know what you do to me?
Sometimes I sit alone and empty
I cry
Why aren't you the way you used to be?
The one who made me feel so warm
just being by my side
But now look in your eyes
It's so cold inside
it just makes me shiver within
Why can't we pretend to be
the way we are in my memories
Maybe we'll just simply forget our aches
Cause I stay awake
I don't even begin to sleep
And if we can't, then I don't wanna remember
when things were good between you and I
Cause' it'll only lead to now when I think
of you and cry

## Alone Again

Out of the cold
into her arms
A heart that's froze
begins to warm
Lost in her endless charm
Beautiful smile
and promise of a future
where I'll never be alone again
Because I've found a home within
her heart
Away from lies and tears
I don't belong with them
I belong with her
My weak heart grows so strong with her
So I give in
when she promises a cure for loneliness
that her love alone can mend
Out of the dark
Into the unknown
No matter how sweet love sounds
it only seems to sing one song –
Heartbreak
No matter how much I've grown to depend
on the warmth of her arms
I'll be out in the cold again
Broke, the same promises told again
Froze again
But for now – tears, hold them in
Enjoy her love, shouting in praise
But doubting the ways
All the while, counting the days
Till I'm alone again

# Sounds Of War

## Sounds Of War

Life's a struggle
The skies are gray
The mic's a hustle
They say,
as I put these rhymes to waste
'ill as shit'
but yall' ain't hearing this
Then I hear some shit
like yall' really feelin' this?
Well maybe I should put mines away
Hip Hop died but we still breathin'
They cool on food for thought
but we still feeding
Beneath the surface flow
Thinkin' if every verse is cold
We could nurture souls
Hell, it don't hurt to grow
but the soil is barren
World full of toil, despair and
desperation

## Lost Soldier

The bullet,
I'm still biting it
Say, "Show heart soldier"
The worst part's over
For some reason, I'm still frightened
The war's over
I feel like I'm still fighting it
Sometimes I don't know how to feel
Somebody pull me from the battlefield
Tell my mother her son's a soldier
She didn't lose her baby to guns or bombs
I'm just growing older
Now I understand why she prayed before and after
meals
Cause' life's a battlefield
Faith teaches you how to feel
We march on, full steam through the hassle
Continue to fight
Even though it may seem like a losing battle
So tell my baby brother his big brother's a soldier
and even with the weight of the world on my back
I still have room for him on my shoulders
I'll go to war so he could live in peace
Or die trying
to give him a reason to live at least
See through our blinding rage
We soldiers living in a time where our minds are caged
Fighting for freedom

# This Encounter

Red Dress
Got me thinking dance floor
Then the bed next
See how far her legs stretch
I mean, she bad
Everything from her toe to her head, blessed
I tell her, I love the way you move
I can see rhythm
P.S, we should kinect
It'll be better than a wii system
She say, I'm talking game and I laugh it off
Cause' I was...but I can pass it off
Now, I'm thinking if her ass if soft
She can make it bounce till it smack the walls
I'll smash
Till her apple bottom makes apple sauce
She say lets get a room, I say that'll cost
And where I be chillin, its mirrors on the ceiling
So we hook up and you just look up
When I say bay, watch like Hasslehoff
Plus, you just ride slow
And when you get the vision
You get the feeling, you giving and living a live show
You got a man? To my surprise, NO
And that's good ya feel me
Cause' when talking dirty lead to something filthy
I don't want you feeling guilty
I want you feeling lifted, ecstasy
Desperately, sexually
Body screaming out, rescue me!
Panting like ya breathe is weak
Till you pass out next to me
And wake up like we should do it again

Cause' you is a ten
But I gotta go
It was so good, should've knew it would end
She said, I probably should forget you
And I said, I better do the same
And she left
I took a breath
Like damn, I never knew her name

## Spoken Word

It's the cries of the people
Lies of the decietful
Disguise of the evil
Rise and I'll teach you
I won't ask to borrow a buck
Just lend me your ear
Water my soul
Send me your tears
Help me grow a seed
that will grow to lead
the new generation of Noah's breed
once the watered down overflows the seas
Serpents and sharks, that's for dreamers
There wasn't an Ark in Katrina
Just an awful stench that lingered
and brought back memories
Still fighting the same wars
that was fought back centuries ago
The world shows no sympathy for the po'
Ghettos sentenced me to the hole
But it's with this energy that I flow
that made my ancestors resist misery on the boat
Spirits to the glorious sky
Raise my pen with a warriors cry
Demand truth, no more of the lies
and we'll make it out alive
Like proud lions, generations out the Pride
This land is our kingdom
Stand tall but crouch low when approaching herds
While cowards choke on the verbs
Never underestimate the power of the Spoken Word

## Happy Together
Drug Symphony

I fell in love with you
We do the same things that lovers do
You fuck me...just not under the covers boo
You fuck my head up
You got me stuffing meds just to get a head rush
Lay'ing in my bed flushed
Eyes rolling back, cries holding back
Buzz died, it's like my love died
Now try consoling that
I'm a widow, but you here though
Just give me a kiss, I shed a tear slow
and watch the smoke disappear...whoa
Love when you with me, I appear whole
Shivering and shaking when you not
I appear cold
Body aching, cause' you my better half
The reason that I'll never have
and end up on a metal slab
Toe tagged – that'll be our wedding band
Til' death do us part baby
Fuck what the reverned saying
They all trying to discove'
Hear mothers crying for their cubs
Why I'm dying for your love?

I'll do anything to have you for the night
I covet you, but loving you's gamble for my life

They say its death I'm wishing on my health
As we kissing, they don't see the addiction
Just the pain I'm inflicing on myself but...
Pain is love, I gotta have it

I got a habit
I'm an addict
Your girls' a beast? I got a savage
I'm in love with, the way she does it
The way the blood rushes to my head
She'll even do it in public
People staring at us like I'm the villian
But her hurt is healing
She helps me fight this worthless feeling
When you dream big, but you see reality is small
Thinking life has more in store for you
but actually, this all
Ya friends left...none of ya ends left
Nothing but the ends left
Waiting til' you can no longer take in breath
Ya lungs seize, ya heart stops
Don't stop suffocating me baby, you got me hard rock
I mean rock hard, I'll never forget
how this feelings' better than sex
Hope I never regret

I'll do anything to have you for the night
I covet you, but loving you's a gamble for my life

We fall asleep wherever; strangers wake us up
It seems like the whole world wanna break us up
Why they interefering? Trying to intervene
They call it intervention; they trying to end a dream
Can't they see you're perfect for me?
If it wasn't worth it I'd be with her, instead of she
And she my ex still
It's less real with a 'X' pill
but I'm scared to leave her...why?
They say my ex kills
Nothing like a woman scorned, can't even plan to leave

She's never abandoned me
She's my only family
I lost everything, my sanity
How can it be?
They calling you a whore, but I see vanity
A prom queen; a bomb fiend, but she's a prostitute
Not just me, I hear its lots of dudes
Stay with me for life, I'll pay for the night
And hope tomorrow never comes
I'm happier with you
Please accept this ring
Just ask me and I do......

## Focus

That's my conscience calling...
But I don't wanna talk now
Shit, he makes my brain itch
talking bout the same shit
"Be Conscious"
Everything'll come to us
Niggas put the gun to us
tried to leave me unconscious
I've been gone, they like damn we miss you
but I'm struggling with family issues
My grandma's gone but still breathing
It's nothing they can do
She forgot how to eat
got her munchin' through a tube
She forgot how to speak
Now they all say I'm stubborn and
I'm scared to call
that's death on the other end
She won't talk back, don't know if
she'll understand
I'm at a loss for words
Nobody understands
All they see is, I don't phone her
Always been a loner
So I tell'em leave me alone
Now, we don't get along
But fuck what my cousins think
Pour me another drink, of potion
I ain't gon' lie...I'm losing focus

# The Come Up

Take it back to the corner
before it was gang turf
where they slang work
Poets used to show what their slangs worth
So the game birthed
prodigies of ghetto policies
The backpacker college breeds
hot as these Chicago streets
You gotta breathe, or else suffocate
Hustle til' ya muscles ache
It's hard waiting, plus starvation
seems like a worser fate
So you grab a couple tapes
Sit up in ya room, speakers on boom
Then BOOM! Ya people on the news
You don't like how the image is
Always acting ignorant
Women lacking dividends
Niggas acting feminine
Poverty brings robbery, robbing sprees
What you suppose to do?
Every other victim seems as broke as you
A lose, lose...that's how you sum up that game
Ya come up'ets steady coming
but the come up ain't came

# My Life

Every night shots go off
Cops go lost
In this concrete jungle
You cannot go soft
It's hard body or get ya squad bodied
See yall probably think I'm exaggerating
We the results of a savage nation
and lack of patience, but what you expect
When they owe but won't cut you a check
It's frustrating, plus too much hating
Most people making enough to just make it
That equals enough waiting
Can you trust Satan?
He promises to rid you of pain
All he asks is your soul in exchange
It's getting real
They threaten to take the one thing you live for
Put guns to your kids, you consider making the deal
Well don't deal with the devil, he's sure to cheat ya
See them snakes there, don't play fair either
It's a lose, lose I guess that's why they hate me
I find a way to win, no matter what the stakes be

## Hip Hop Saved Me

Let's be real, I write for my fee
I write to make it right, don't like how I eat
Life in these streets ain't the life that I need
But it's putting food on the table
so who gonna save you?
It ain't like I want a stunna chain
Shit, I'm under strain
It's a wonder what people will do
to avoid hunger pains
It's real when ya stomach ache
Feelin' like you gonna break
You a runaway
No home, so where you gonna stay
Mind just run astray
Fought, but you see you loss
Full of evil thoughts
Can't escape, can't sleep it off
What you expect then? Stressed
and pressure becomes ya best friend
Way closer than ya next kin
Try to get on the right path, finish a song
But can only write half
Before you dealt another one of life's jabs
Want mils from a label; another starving artist
No deals on the table, but bills on the table
So every day, go punch a clock
and try to freestyle something hot
Better than going back to a nothing block
Where the only thing waiting for you is Hell
They all waiting for you to fail
Well, let that hate motivate you to excel

Just had a dream, I was laying in a hearst

Skipped to being homeless man...laying in the dirt
So no wonder why I work
and creep when no one else up
Cause' I rather miss sleep
than have to sleep in a shelter
Hustle up to earn, if the early bird gets it
I'm up before the worm
Need enough of it to burn
I try to live smart, pops told me to buy stock
But it's beef on my block, so my people buy glocks
It ain't the safest place to stay
Try to live smart but why live for tomorrow
if you don't make it through today
Say we take it the grave, I don't wanna die young
but we rarely see the good ever make it to old age
Before we take it to the stage, let's all say a prayer
for the emcees we lost just so we could be here
The hard road traveled...Big, Pac I pray for
Hip Hop saved me, I'm returning the favor

## Sunshine

Probably ain't seen it
A lot of people sleeping
Say, "Nah, he ain't decent"
and probably ain't mean it
America got a scheme
You probably ain't dream it
That's the reason the view out your window
probably ain't scenic
Even them country boys can tell you what it's like
Poverty's a monopoly, they tell you that it's life
But if you can rhyme words
and they tell you that it's nice
They'll tell you sell ya soul and help you with advice
Now you become an image, cause' we admire niggaz
Higher learning,
Your soul yearning for the highest bidder
Now sit and try n' figure, who the pimp and who the
ho'?
Cause' you a hustler, but getting pimped through the
door
Sent to the store, and you can't really explain that
All you really know is you better bring they change back
You don't see the options cause' you was starving, frail
Before this lil bit of shine, it was dark as hell

Too much Bacardi, now they callin' you naughty
Seems like yesterday, you was playing with ya Barbies
Pushing across the floor; dream car a Ferrari
Thinking material things can put you where the stars be
Quit school, hittin' the books don't pay
Bet, but don't forget good looks go a long way
That's what she's thinking as her song play
and he trying to hold her ass, asking for her photograph

"You got potential baby!
Come with me, let's talk about your credentials baby!"
No role model
but thought she'd hit the road, model
Told her to pose hollow
Clothes on the floor followed...more bottles
"You oh so cute!"
While he sexing her
She forgot this was supposed to be a photo shoot
She's sho no groupie, thinking she should scream rape
But then she's just a tease, he got the whole thing on
tape

The days gon' get better
But for now, just seems like they gon' get wetter
It's coming down and when it rains, it pours
And since we all Gods' children, my pain is yours
Heard'em say, it's no good in these streets
I wasn't the son that got shot
but it could've been me
It could've been my brother, cousin, or friend
Me trying to save'em, blood covering my Tims
Cause' of thugs muggin' the brim of my fitted hat
Reason enough to take a life? What kind of shit is that!?
Once it's gone you'll never get it back
The trigger lapsed, now you gotta live with that
Conscious against you
Now you can't sleep, thinking the monsters will get you
The cost of the heartless
Wish you could've thought up some smart shit
before you got lost in the darkness

# Immortalize

A picture can capture essence
Even when I'm long gone
Never again to be in your presence
You can forever hold my present
In the blink of an eye, I can vanish
And yet I'm still standing by your side
like I never said goodbye
It's like a flower
that will wait forever to bloom
A sense of warmth and happiness
that never leaves a room
A dream that ends, but hopes continue to fly
A man whose life begins and he never seems to die
The passion that will live on
after your withered age and dying day
The imprint that I've made
I pray the ink will never leave this page

# My Tomorrow

Where is a mind to go for homage,
when today you realize your tomorrow's not promised?
For every soul that was blessed enough to awake
there's an unfortunate one that won't see the end of
today
That's why at the beginning, we pray
Today's epic is hollow and I predict a sorrow
that will depict our tomorrow
In the deepest stare of hatred's eyes
we're doomed to never see clear skies again
Make no amends and condemn us
Follow trends where we lose many of family and friends
with the struggles that never end
Maybe one day I can look back and I'll laugh
I'll be glad to surpass the negativities that never see
their last
If my story turns out to be rags to riches, sign Prolific
Carried through my hard times with my rhymes
I'd carry them with pride and never disguise my stitches
Cause' for every day I was down, disguised and strained
It gave me another reason to rise high, hopefully over
the pain
I thought of all I could gain when I had nothing to lose
If I changed my mind frame, I'd have nothing to prove
Why pressure myself with the stress of always trying to
impress
someone else with less, when this is only to express
myself
I can only live my life for me and that's only how I live
life free

## Restless

I will walk this road alone
for my soul has no abode
And my heart has not found one
for which I can share the burden of this load

I will walk this road alone
for my soul has no abode
And my heart has not found one
in which my feelings may console

I am restless
My life may never go on
As the days go by
Until I seize her love
To ease my suffering
Nothing in this world will be enough
Nor will my soul find a peaceful place to lie
And like my love for her
I will never die

Have you ever loved?
Then you know what it's like to cherish

Have you ever been loved?
Then you know what it's like
to feel warmth even in the harsh of a cold night
Or in the darkest of despair, find an array of light
And for that descended light to transcend
and leave you alone
When your heart has been abandoned
and that persons' love is gone

## Understand My Pain

Dear lord, I know I don't pray often
but understand my hurting
I speak with you today in pain
hoping you will soften my burden
Cushion my fall
I stand alone in a world of opposition
and at times, I admit, I don't stand tall
Which is a shame
Cause' I know I'll always have you backing me
But at times I'm lacking the...
Courage and ambition from the roots in which I came
Lacking the...
Confidence and pride, hence I call your name
Dear God, understand my pain
For I don't understand it myself
There are children born never to be hugged
Born to be misjudged
Born into a world they've never met, that holds a
grudge
When I thought we were born to be loved
Sometimes I ponder, did even you expect this?
A being of your perfection and greatness couldn't have
been mistaken
Or did you purposely create this?
I can't say I never cry but my tears I often hold back
In my heart, strength resides and I thank you for that
I don't mean to pry, but when people younger than I die
What was their lives worth?
The life of your son was percious, though he was
accused and slain
Could any of our lives be the same, if we weren't abused
and chained?

Good or bad, I try to believe that everything happens for
a reason
Until the bad happens to me and I feel you've committed
a treason
I understand that I am a part of your perfect plan
to collide and divide humans, and decide the truth that
lies in man
For your creations, spread the innovation of
unconditional love
And in the binds of hardship, we may rise above
Once again return to the paradise this land once became
Reminisce on the days we had no choice but to
withstand harsh rains
And maybe with you, we will understand that pain
                                        Amen

## Life Is...

Somebody tell me what life is
Life is...
My pain
A desert terrain watered by my tears
Where I try to bury the pain
Still it remains
And I sustain just like this...
writing what life is

## When A Dream Dies

Parents cry
The streets claim lives
You lose sight of all hope
but before that...direction
All of us sigh
It's hard to watch an angel fall from the sky
When a dream dies
You'll do anything on a slight dare
And now you've become the monster
of your own nightmare
since no more does life care
It only spurns the hate more
And since it's taught you such harsh lessons
you return the favor
When a dream dies
No one can break your spirits
I hope you feel my truths
And take heed to your dreams...
They can only be killed by you

## Prolific...I AM

It's the knowledge of the youth untold
Our roots un-grown, so when the truth unfolds
You will realize and know it's me
I told you my story through the eyes of poetry
I ran for the light, darkness soon banned from my life
And I'd be damned for the strife
But I'm as deep as my words, so I AM what I write

## Nail In The Coffin

Weren't you my friend?
Now I'm here to bury you
Alive, but dead to me

## We At War

My cousins' at war
One country's need
One man's greed to feed
his lust for power
Fulfill the dreams
a past him couldn't clutch for ours
My brothers' at war
Cause' another fool dissed him
Acting too hard in the schoolyard
so he feud and threw fist at'em
Mentality of the kids in the public school system
My mother's at war
Trying to stay strong enough to raise a bolder
and amidst the struggle, still raise a soldier
Sometimes I feel like I have no way to console her
All I can do is hug you
tell you I love you
and pay a bill for you
Just know that I'd slay and kill for you
My family's at war
We slowly growing apart
Not as tight as when we were kids
Growing is hard
My friend's at war
They don't like me no more
Now they want beef, want to take it to the streets
My Grandmother's at war
She's fighting a mental disease
Doctors say as it gets worse she won't even remember
me
Grandma, remember we lived in better times
There may have been tears of joy but it was never
crying

Now you shed tears for your boys doing several crimes
Just trying to survive but we can do better with our
clever minds
Defend the weak and feed the poor
All we need is peace to cease the war
I wish we can see that more
But until that day, I guess we'll just be at war

## And Still I Write

What's in my blood
Somewhere becomes a part of my soul
Cause' what seems everlasting
I have a passion for that never grows old
When confronted with some of life's problems
My temporary solution is to write
I don't know if I'm right or wrong
but there can come no harm when I write
I express my strength with ink
that spills dark but spreads light
My pen becomes my only weapon
in life's day to day fight
Some I win, often I may lose
And still I write

## My Worst Enemy

My worst enemy has no face
It has no place, yet can't be erased
It has no ground on which to stand
But will devour, conquer, and walk over any man
There is no air for it to breathe
Yet it can suffocate you
or just as easily bring you to your knees
How it survives, sustains, and remains...
Is only because I believe
My beliefs throw gas on the flames, until it is ash
Because my worst enemy doesn't exist in you
It can...but then it'd become your worst enemy too
The wars that we have, I pray for them to end
Because hate makes me the only casualty
And the real wars are being fought within

## I Only Hear Sirens

I only hear sirens
Mothers crying
Brothers hiding
Like death cares about us dying
The streets paved with chalk
Nowhere to walk in innocence
Nowhere where darkness diminishes
Bodies drop and nobody stops
Many of us keep moving
while plenty of lives we're losing
Time never misses a tock, and guns cock
The sound reminds me of the ones before
Such horrors don't matter
Only the sound that suddenly comes after
Echoed with the shiesty grins of men
with shady laughter

## Why?

I cried last night
Why?
I know somebody who died last night
Why?
Another, took another's man's life
Why?
Maybe, because of the struggles of his own life
Why?
Still that's no reason to be as cold as stone
Why?
It's still wrong, but the life he took wasn't his own
Why?
That's an answer I can't give to anyone else
Why?
Cause I'm still awaiting the answer from God to know
myself
Why?
It was he who birthed us children in this world,
where most of us won't have the chance to grow
Why?
I don't know

## Cold In Your Arms

To ask such a question would be somewhat bold of me
But as I'm holding you and you're holding me...
Do you feel a cold in me?
I'm always there for her when she needs love
but when my heart aches, I wait...
Guess I care more for her than she does...for me
And unfortunately,
I'd give her my last breath for a moment of her affection
or whatever she has left...for me
I understand it takes a part of your heart and it's hard
each time
When your beliefs dying and they leave you crying,
falling apart
Sometimes I doubt when she says she loves me
Just the touch of her lips couldn't be considered much of
a kiss
I feel the cold chill when she un-wraps me from each
hug at the door
as she's leaving...I doubt she loves me anymore
And I pray that the feeling is wrong
Yet I'm holding her in my arms and still feeling alone
I fear what to expect but I'm not here for regret
At once our love was whole...now I'm loving a silhouette
Does she still care? Could she share with me the
awww's?
But I'm so cold in your arms...like you're not there with
me at all

## The Gauntlet

I been abandoned by the hordes, stranded by shores
Branded by the wars, just a man and his sword
Dripping the blood of a victim, but no remorse in me
It wasn't my choice to be...I too was forced to bleed
They torched the trees of my birthplace, I was forced to
leave
into a worse place, beaten and treated like I wasn't
worth grace
They tortured me, hoping that I'd be broken by the
chambers
Provoked by the strangers, as I'd hang up soaked by the
anger
Chambers were threshold dark, I'm envisioning my
mind break
My flesh holds scars, they're only conditioning my mind
state
They didn't want a sane man; the plan was to form an
insane clan
of animalistic killers of niggers for this cannibalistic
thriller
I was the best at it; a flesh savage but I felt I had loss
though
My thoughts froze...how do you define victory to a lost
soul?
Survival isn't victory, cause us survivors couldn't free
our seeds
Or say "We are fee" – so victory is defined as just a song
by B.I.G
We mourn and produced few strong, they knew we'd
choose wrong
Though they didn't like that plan, they let us loose as
living proof

we'd fail without a righteous hand in the gauntlet...life
of a black man

## When I See Fame

When I see fame
I'll know that I've seen change
and it was worth the grief, the belief
that my dreams weren't out of range
Myself, I'll never doubt again
I hope I don't see sorrow and fear
That nonsense here that brings constant tears
Things that'll leave a man soul feeling beat down
Despair, lack of care, hopelessness as I approach the end
The same things I seem to see now
So I can look back on when I used to see frowns
I hope I don't see shame, fingers pointing the blame
Closest friends disappointed, I don't remember their
names
I hope I don't see myself somewhere gone of my soul
Alone on this road, when I see fame

## Greatest Feeling

As sweet as a rose
As deep as the prose
the greatest of poets once spoke
So to believe that it's heard
My words won't fall on deaf ears
I'd speak with the words
the greatest of poets once wrote
I'd give you a sight of how life is without her
So maybe you'll know what it's like
if I don't show it just right –
the feeling I get just writing about her
And if I wrote to be bold, I only hope to be told
by someone that the words spoke to their soul
Heals the hearts the greatest of fools once broke
With the promising words to give to the hurt
Give them the worth of those who only want hope
Lift the heads of the lowest and homes to the poorest
Cease the rain and bring peace to the pain
To be known as one of those poets –
gives me the greatest feeling

## Nothin' In These Streets

What will it be?
What will it be?

I admit that I wouldn't listen, I was on a mission
If your feelings had went missing, I wouldn't miss it
Day and night in the streets, we stayed right in the streets
till daylight then we strayed like we were thieves
I crawled in the bed with you like seven in the morning
How you slept with the annoyance
I missed several different warnings
that you were tired of it
Getting expired loving
from your aspired husband
And I would get fired up when
You'd argue and complain
like 'are you gonna change?'
But we're arguing in vain, it's just strange

What will it be...

Me or the streets?
And I keep laughing
It's no time for jokes, we goin' broke
but you keep asking

What will it be...

Can't you see we need money
but not more than you need me
And if need be, I'd leave it alone
But then where would my seed be?
Screaming 'who's gonna feed me?' –

If daddy ain't home
But I'm glad he ain't home
He never could see
that there was nothin' in these streets
but the weeps and griefs
Insanity man
How struggles turn out a cold hustla
from a family man
Damn, now the whole family's praying
that you'll soon see
that besides home, there's nothin' you need
And there's nothin' in these streets

## 60 Seconds Of Heaven

Roads were slippery, it was too late by time I seen the
bright lights
I heard my baby scream in faded dreams and gleams of
white light
Then I heard her say, "I do", standing there in her white
dress
Asked if she's the one I want to spend the rest of my life
with..."Yes"
The time was perfect and just to marry a dime was
worth it
but I felt like my mind was jerking in and out of reality
Cause' I could her voices scream, "In and out, you gotta
breathe!"
A look into my wife's face, her smile puts me back in the
right place
A honeymoon two flights away, too nice and we had two
nights to stay
Came back home and wrote about it – me, her and her
carrying my seed
I carry the lead on best sellers, so the next book they in
a hurry to read
I was too nervous to breathe, watching her give birth to
my seed
I blacked out – "Keep pushing, I won't lose him. This'll
work I believe"
My grandma was the first to hold the baby and I was
told that maybe
it's not mine; then I grew cold and shaky and replied,
"Stop lying"
Voices screaming, "Don't stop trying, he's coming
around"
My whole world was crumbling now, happiness was
coming to frowns

My wife had nothing to say so I just slumped and I prayed
Said, "Grandma but we just buried you," it's been a month and a day
Everybody faded away and I laid on my back on the concrete
Strange voices saying to me, "Hey, just stay calm and breathe"
Both cars wrecked and everybody dead that was in it except me
I was just dead for a minute

## New Day Soldiers

We rise and you chant us
Born from the pride of the Panthers
New day soldiers
Move weight soldiers
No mountain is too strong to move
Go against us
there's no doubt you're going to lose
New day soldiers, too strong to cry
Been surviving way too long to die now
Or lie down
New day soldiers
Leaders of our dynasty like a new Jay Hova
Sentence me to darkness, they will send you the light
Never give up; a new soldier will continue the fight

# Retire My Mic

When my ink runs dry
and my ear drums die
so I no longer hear the beat
I'll retire my mic
When my flow stops illin'
and my soul stops feelin'
There's no music left in me
I'll retire my mic
Say it's been a good run
Sorry, I could cry
Won't be a long goodbye
when I retire my mic

## A Road Uncharted

I ask for direction or any advice you may have
but there's not a soul to know on this road as I pass
I haven't seen a sign to guide me, which way do I go?
Who'll ever find me? I could be lost and don't know
Soon it turns dark and I spew in fright
A few have walked before me
and yet I see no signs of human life
Not a footprint made for each step they prevailed
Only the gravesites of those who've tried and failed
These signs of discouragement lead me to believe
there has to be some sign of hope that I'll succeed
As I find myself further lost in an abyss
I fear that I've already passed that sign and I missed it
Though there are no excuses – it's a threat to my future
I've traveled from a boy to a man
from a scheme to a plan
It's useless, if those who follow me fail to understand
that life is a road that tempts you with wrong turns
Most of us will walk alone, and some fall off
Stay straight and keep the faith in the path you walk
states the only known sign on the road uncharted

## Beautiful Mind

What is peace?
The streets are shattered
Peace is the end of matter
The end of people asking,
Can I have a –
If I don't have it, then yall gotta forgive
Cause' people say I got it
but I don't got it to give
And it's nothing I would love more
than to take us all above poor
Throw up a couple dubs for
all the people I got love for
Take a bottle of bub, pour
Let's make a toast
Now where we headed? What's ya fetish?
Let's take a vote
And we can fly where the people shine
But for now, this piece of mines
is the only way I get peace of mind
Sleepless firing
Stray bullet in his arm – shock!
That'll wake him up, don't need an alarm clock
We at war – just waiting till the bombs drop
Makes you wonder what it was like on Saddam's block
I wonder if the beef will ever cease yall
If we products of our environment
then we need a recall


What's really goin' on?
Sometimes
it feels like the whole city's goin' wrong
But we steady goin' strong

Cause it's futile trying
When you trying
to stop the shine of a beautiful mind

## Blizzard Blues

Flakes turn to frost
Wind of the night whispers
Icicles, crushed...crisp
Touch lips
and melt away...light kisses
Goodnight wishes
Close your eyes, you might miss it
Cold skies
Black night, bold dyes
A billion white holes dive
like the night told lies
Little white lies, lose innocence
when beautiful fall
doesn't dissolve, but grew inches
Emotional pile up
Trying to create a love potion I'm proud of
But I'm stuck in madness
Lusting habits got me stuck in traffic
Had to abandon the old me
I'm just standing, stranded in cold freeze
So I'm walking and my eyes found
So many abandoned hearts, they shut the drive down
In the distance, a faint crying sound
but I can't hear her
As I shiver, wish I was near her
but can my cold heart give her more than a blizzard
I'm stressing over past ish
Wish I didn't have to drag it, wish I left it
Now to get my message that I love you
You just gotta shovel through the baggage of my exes
For our sake try, I know it's waist high
Two feet and fallin' thick
We too deep to call it quits

I come to you, comfort you cause it's so warm
No where else I'd rather be in a snow storm
We'll dig our way out
Something I hope and pray bout
Even though it's cold and gray out
Still, the flowers may sprout
Could say this is real love but who really knows
When all was lost, it seemed
You defrosted me while the city froze

## ABOUT THE AUTHOR

Fidel M. Love was born on the southside of Chicago, IL. He is a graduate of East-West University with a Bachelors degree in English & Communications. He has been writing poetry and fiction since age 12 and is currently seeking to pursue his Masters degree in Creative Writing.

www.ingramcontent.com/pod-product-compliance
Lightning Source LLC
Chambersburg PA
CBHW060743050426
42449CB00008B/1292

* 9 7 8 0 6 1 5 6 3 3 2 4 4 *